While yelling a warning at Captain Wainwright, I flung my sword towards the cowardly rascal perched above us. Round and round it whirled, whistling like the blades of the windmill on Clifton Heights in a brisk sou'wester.

The Frenchie, realizing too late what was going to happen, opened his mouth to scream. No sound came. Instead, a few seconds later, his javelin clattered harmlessly to the deck. Shortly afterwards his severed head thudded heavily down beside it and rolled awkwardly into the gunwales.

As a reward for saving his life, the captain set me ashore in Plymouth with a hearty farewell and a leather bag containing twenty guineas. 'Make good use of it, John Blanke,' he said kindly. 'Make something of yourself, for you are a man of no ordinary talents.'

D1434439

www.kidsatrandomhouse.co.uk

Also by Stewart Ross:

Pirates, Plants and Plunder

Written by Stewart Ross

GREED, SEEDS
AND
SLAVERY

Illustrated by
David Roberts

Eden Project Books

GREED, SEEDS AND SLAVERY
AN EDEN PROJECT BOOK 978 1 905 81108 3

Published in Great Britain by Eden Project Books,
an imprint of Transworld Publishers

This edition published 2007

1 3 5 7 9 10 8 6 4 2

Text copyright © Stewart Ross, 2007
Illustrations copyright © David Roberts, 2007

The right of Stewart Ross to be identified as the author of
this work has been asserted in accordance with the Copyright,
Designs and Patents Act 1988.

All rights reserved. No part of this publication may be reproduced,
stored in a retrieval system, or transmitted in any form or by
any means, electronic, mechanical, photocopying, recording or
otherwise, without the prior permission of the publishers.

Set in 11.5/17pt Sabon
by Falcon Oast Graphic Art

TRANSWORLD PUBLISHERS
61–63 Uxbridge Road, London W5 5SA

www.kidsatrandomhouse.co.uk
www.edenproject.com

Addresses for companies within The Random House Group Limited
can be found at: www.randomhouse.co.uk/offices.htm

THE RANDOM HOUSE GROUP Limited Reg. No. 954009

A CIP catalogue record for this book is available
from the British Library.

The Random House Group Limited supports The Forest Stewardship
Council® (FSC®), the leading international forest-certification organisation.
Our books carrying the FSC label are printed on FSC®-certified paper.
FSC is the only forest-certification scheme supported by the leading
environmental organisations, including Greenpeace. Our
paper procurement policy can be found at
www.randomhouse.co.uk/environment

Printed and bound in Great Britain by Clays Ltd, St Ives PLC

GREED, SEEDS
AND
SLAVERY

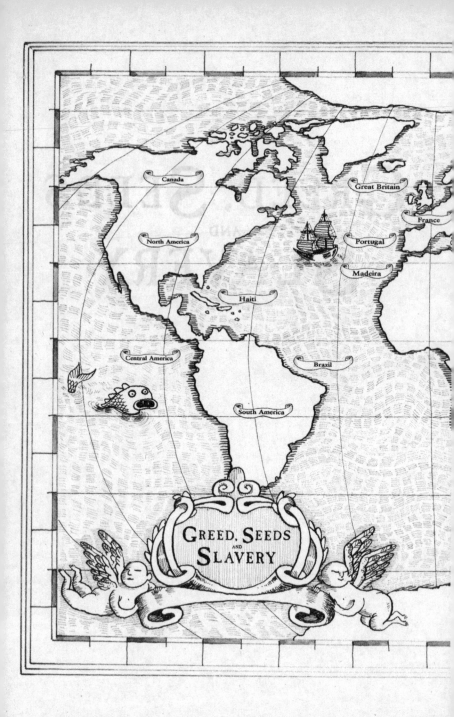

Canada

Great Britain

France

North America

Portugal

Madeira

Haiti

Central America

Brazil

South America

GREED, SEEDS
AND
SLAVERY

CONTENTS

Thomas Pellow

It all began back in 1715. There I was, sitting in the schoolroom in Penryn, Cornwall, scratching my head and wondering what all this Latin meant and dreaming of being out of school and on the open sea with the wind in my hair and—

'Pellow! I asked you a question! Will you be good enough to answer it, boy?'

It was old 'Flogger' Travis, schoolmaster and bane of my life for the last year and a half. Did I know the answer to his question? I didn't

1

even know what the question was! So I got a slap about the ears and six strokes of the cane across my backside and was told that I was the dullest pupil he had ever taught. I knew he didn't mean it because the previous week my friend Jack Barnecutt had been awarded Flogger's worst-ever badge. Be that as it may, the beating confirmed what I had known for several weeks: that schooling was a waste of time – all I really wanted was to be a sailor.

Of course, my parents wouldn't agree, so I tackled my sea-faring uncle, John Pellow. He was about to sail to Genoa, Italy, with a cargo of pilchards and I begged him, day and night, to let me sail with him. Finally he agreed and spoke with my parents. I have never seen a more unhappy pair than my mama and papa were that evening. They wept and wrung their hands and pleaded with me to reconsider. But all their talk of discomfort and danger passed clean over my head – I hadn't a clue what they were on about. After listening to their warnings and advice for well over an hour, I was eventually asked whether I still wanted to sail with Uncle John. Well, I replied that of course I did!

Oh, the stupidity of youth! Why didn't I

listen? Why had God given me such kind parents who, instead of ordering me not go to sea, left the decision to their ignorant, hot-headed son? Dearest Mama, please forgive me! I know now how right you and Papa were when you begged me to stay at home. I regret what I did – regret it with all my heart and lost soul!

We sailed on a Monday afternoon. By the following morning I would have given my right hand to be back in Flogger's safe, cosy classroom. Not only was Uncle John far stricter than old Flogger in keeping me to my books, but his punishment for slacking was not the single rod of the cane but the many-headed lash of the cat-o'-nine-tails. Worse still, any free time I was allowed was not spent playing, as it would have been during the school day, but clambering to the top of the mainmast in all weathers and sitting, or rather clinging, there as the ship's lookout. I was sick, frozen, hungry, sore and generally more miserable than I had ever been in my life. Although but ten years old, I didn't dare weep, either, in case some member of the crew saw my tears and reported me to Uncle John for being of a feeble nature – which would have resulted in yet another flogging.

I endured all this suffering and did not throw myself into the sea because I believed that in a few weeks I would be back again in the kindly care of dear Flogger Travis. Alas! Had I known what was about to happen to me, I believe I would have done anything to end my wretched life immediately.

We had unloaded our stinking cargo in Genoa and, with our hold full of some fancy cloth that Uncle believed would sell well in England, were well on our way home when from the masthead I spied two strange ships making towards us at great speed. No sooner had the captain raised his spyglass to see what type of vessels were approaching than I was urgently called down to the deck and told to get out of sight. The sailors referred to our unwanted visitors as 'Sallee Rovers'. This, I soon learned to my horror, meant they were pirates from North Africa!

We didn't stand a chance. Our enemy was more numerous, faster and better armed than us. Cowering below decks, I heard the most dreadful sounds as first the Rovers fired cannon at us, smashing two masts, then drew alongside and charged aboard in huge numbers. I imagine some of our men put up a fight because I saw much blood on the deck when I emerged. Resistance was fruitless, however, and soon our crew was divided between the two Rover ships and locked away in the holds without food, water or sunlight.

Now, after weeks of biting my lip, I finally allowed myself to cry. I howled like a dog at first, then quietened to continuous sobbing that lasted all that long, long night. Mother, father, friends, the little town of Penryn, the beautiful Cornish countryside, my England – I had lost for ever all that had been closest to my young, broken heart. Along with the sailors who sat in silence beside me, I was doomed to a life of slavery.

For a full month we survived as prisoners of Admiral Abdul Rahman Medune, commander of our prison ship. Each of us was inspected early on – the admiral wanting to know exactly what his plunder was worth – and occasionally kicked to make sure we were still alive, but then we saw no one but the surly fellow who brought us our daily ration of bread and water.

Our inactivity ended the moment we arrived at the Sallee base of Rabat. No sooner had we dropped anchor than a great cry of 'Garnoe! Garnoe!' came from the deck above. 'Garnoe', we quickly learned, was the local version of 'Delgarno', the name of a much-feared British naval captain whose job it was to root out piracy. Captain Delgarno, it seems, had followed us to Rabat and was now preparing to attack the Sallee ships. Admiral Medune panicked, cut his anchor ropes and made a dash for the open sea. He forgot that the tide had gone out and we were soon stuck on a sandbank at the harbour entrance, a sitting target for Delgarno's cannon.

In a short time our ship was smashed to splinters and, being unable to swim, I managed to escape only by clinging to a broken mast. As luck – or Almighty God – would have it, I did not drift out to sea and rescue by the Royal Navy. Instead, the current carried me back to the shore, where I was immediately recaptured. You will not be surprised to hear that my tears returned as copious as before.

My only slight pleasure at this time was to find myself in the same prison as Uncle John who, with much apology, said how sorry he was that he had recommended to my parents that I go away to sea with him. I thanked him for his kindness but said it was too late to do anything about it now. With a sigh of sincere regret, he agreed and said we should both have remembered the wise old proverb: *Better the devil you know than the one you don't*. I was not sure I had ever believed that Flogger Travis was a devil, but the saying certainly made good sense.

After a few days in prison we went inland to the town of Meknes, crossing wild country inhabited by lions and other terrifying creatures. About a mile from the gates, those of us who still had English shoes were ordered to take them off and put on strange yellow slippers. A huge crowd of citizens turned out to greet us. As we walked down the narrow streets between high walls of baked mud, we were spat at and called 'infidel dogs' because we were not Muslims. We were taken to the Old Palace, to appear before the Emperor Ishmael, who paid fifty silver coins for each of us. Only Admiral Medune, who had somehow survived the battle with Captain Delgarno, did not receive anything. Instead, he paid for his cowardice by having his head chopped off with one swipe of a gigantic sword. I was not sorry to see it go.

For a few months I worked in the palace armoury, cleaning and polishing the emperor's large stock of rather old-fashioned weapons. This work was not too bad as I was with English and French sailors who had been captured at the same time as me, and we were able to chat and share a few laughs together. By now I should have known, however, that things were only likely to get worse.

For some reason the emperor removed me from the armoury and gave me as a present to his favourite son, Muley Spah. This young man might have been adored by his father, but he certainly wasn't by me. I have rarely met a more vile dog. To begin with he amused himself by making me run behind him when he went out riding, saying that if I became a Muslim, he would give me a horse as fine as his. When I refused to abandon the Christian religion in which I had been raised, he fastened me with great irons so that I could not move and proceeded to torture me for several months. He began with beatings, screaming 'Confess! Confess!' as the blows rained down on me. Then came the burnings.

Day after day, flames were held against my arms, legs and feet so that I was sick with the smell of my own roasting flesh. This became so intolerable that in the end I had a secret conversation with God in which I asked Him if He would understand if I changed my religion to avoid such terrible pain. I believe God replied that He understood, and I held up a finger to Muley Spah indicating that I surrendered. He roared in delight.

As a Muslim, I was expected to learn Arabic. To help me do this, the emperor, who had always been fond of me, arranged for me to go to school. So here I am, sitting on a bench, trying to learn a difficult foreign language and being shouted at by a fierce schoolmaster.

I've been here before, haven't I? And, yes, I wish I were somewhere else. But this time I think I'll stay put. After all, better the devil you know . . .

THOMAS PELLOW AND WHITE SLAVES
This story is based on the true adventures of Thomas Pellow (born 1705), which he described

in his book, The History of the Long Captivity and Adventures of Thomas Pellow in South Barbary . . . Written by Himself *(1739). A Cornish boy, Thomas was captured and held as a slave in North Africa for twenty-three years before managing to escape. Although his story is more extraordinary than most, it was not unusual for European men and women captured by Arabs to be sold as slaves. If young and good-looking, they were worth a lot of money. Indeed, on occasion Arab slavers actually raided the coasts of northern Europe in search of suitable victims.*

William Wilberforce

All my life I worked for Mr Wilberforce, and now he's gone I won't work for anyone else. I couldn't. He was the best, kindest master a servant could wish for. I know the Lord God don't make saints nowadays, but if he did, I reckon he'd start with Mr Wilberforce. Everyone that man met he treated the same, from the lords in Parliament to the maid who swept his grate every morning.

Listen, I'll tell you a story to show what I mean. It comes from 1833, at the very end of his life, when he was in Sloane Street, London, and almost gone to Heaven.

I remember the day exactly. It was the 26th of July in the year he died. Mr Wilberforce was very ill indeed. He had lain in bed all day, hardly moving. To keep the air clean, although it was high summer, we left the fire burning in the room. The family took it in turns to sit with him, holding his hand and trying to get him to take sips of water from a sponge they held to his lips. I was there as chambermaid, attending to the wishes of everyone, and I wouldn't have had it any other way. Being of use was what I was born for. To my honour, Mr Wilberforce noticed this. 'God bless you, Alice!' he said once. 'If all the world was peopled with Alices, we should none of us want for anything!'

Late in the evening the bell rang downstairs. Five minutes later a tall gentleman dressed in black entered the bedroom. He had come from Parliament, he said, and brought good news. The law to abolish slavery in Britain and all our lands overseas had been accepted by the House of Commons.

Stooping down, he told this to Mr Wilberforce. The old man opened his eyes and smiled. 'Excellent!' he said in a voice not much more than a whisper. 'No more slavery! Thanks be to God!'

'The tree has born the sweetest fruit at last,' said the Parliament gentleman, speaking in a poetical kind of way I only half understood.

'Yes,' replied Mr Wilberforce. 'And do you know when it all began, sir?'

The visitor said he did not.

'Then I will tell you,' continued the invalid. 'Listen, sir. And you, Alice. You are important, too, you know.'

Obeying a signal from Mrs Wilberforce, I joined the family gathered round the bed and heard what the great man had to say.

'I was eight years old when I first went to school,' he began. 'The grammar school in Kingston-upon-Hull, it was, a fine old establishment then run by two brothers, Joseph and Isaac Milner. I was, I suppose, not like most of the other pupils. For a start, I was younger and smaller and I did not much enjoy the rough and tumble of the games field. On one occasion the bigger boys even used me as their football, kicking me towards first one goal and then the other. A particularly large boy – Roland, his name was – kicked me so hard that I was actually lifted off the ground and flew through the air before landing on my hands and knees, cutting myself badly on the flints. I was much upset and shed many tears, as did my dear mother when she heard what had happened.

'In the schoolroom, however, it was very different. Within those four panelled walls the grace of Almighty God lifted up the football and changed it into a bright star. Mr Joseph Milner, who taught us reading and writing, became my admirer and introduced me to many fine works. I read the Holy Bible from cover to cover and learned much of it by heart. The plays of Shakespeare I consumed like sweetmeats, as I did the works of classical authors in both Latin and Greek.

'But Mr Joseph was not content that we read such works to ourselves. "No man can consider himself educated," he often said, "unless he can discourse in public." To that end, he insisted that we all read out loud in clear, bright voices and then explain to our audience the meaning of what we had read.

'Poor Roland was very bad at this. He stuttered and spluttered over the simplest passages, throwing the rest of us into paroxysms of laughter. When it came to talking about the passage he had mangled, he usually did not know where to begin. Once, when asked about the family name of King Henry the Fifth, he said he thought it was Vernon because he was usually referred to as "Henry V"! He received such a thrashing for that, I am surprised he did not run away. The world is most unjust to beat boys who cannot learn, as it would be to beat those who cannot sing or shoot arrows straight. God made us all different and it is not for us to judge his handiwork.

'As I said, reading was my talent. So that the other boys should learn from my performances, Mr Joseph used to set me on a table when it was my turn to read. That way, he said, the others would look up to a sound example. I was kept on high after I had finished so that the others might hear what I had to say about what I had read. One such commentary changed my life for ever.

'I had delivered the story of the Good Samaritan, about an injured traveller who had been rescued

by a total stranger after those who should have known better had left him to die.

'"And now tell us, Wilberforce, what this parable means," Mr Joseph had demanded.

'Thinking for a moment, I said that the story showed how we were all brothers. "God instructs us all to care for one another," I explained in my piping child's voice.

'"Are there no exceptions – not one in all the wide world, Wilberforce?" enquired Mr Joseph grandly.

'"No, sir," I replied. Then, thinking of something that had happened to me recently, I continued, "That means black people as well as white ones."

'The boys around me let out a terrible groan and Mr Joseph slapped his hand to his brow in a gesture of unspeakable horror. "Black people?" he repeated. "Are you saying we should love black people?"

'"Yes, sir. The other day, without realizing it, I dropped half a crown in the street. A black sailor who happened to be passing saw what had happened, picked up the coin and gave it back to me. He was acting like the Good Samaritan."

'"Wilberforce," screamed Mr Joseph, "are you suggesting that the Good Samaritan was a black man?"

'"He may have been, sir. The Bible does not tell us."

'I was grabbed by the collar and beaten there and then for blasphemy. It was the only time I was caned in all my schooldays and I have never forgotten it, dear friends, never.'

Exhausted by the effort of telling the story, Mr Wilberforce lay back on his pillows and closed his eyes.

'You see how God moves in mysterious ways,' he said eventually, his mouth lifting into a weak smile. 'Later, when I had finished my studies and was wondering how I could do God's work, I recalled that beating and why it had been given. Then I knew at once what I had to do. Since we are all – black and white, young and old, rich and poor, learned and unlearned – made in the image of the Almighty, we have no right to enslave one half of humanity, one half of God's creation. It was my life's duty to point this out and end the injustice of slavery.

'And now my work is all but completed, I can depart in peace to meet my maker.'

At that point I broke into such tears that I had to leave the room. Those were the last words as I heard Mr Wilberforce utter. Two days later – God rest his soul! – he was dead.

WILLIAM WILBERFORCE

William Wilberforce (1759–1833), a British politician of strong Christian principles, was one of his country's greatest humanitarian reformers. He devoted his life and much of his fortune to ending slavery in British lands. Thanks largely to his tireless campaigning, the slave trade in British ships was made illegal in 1807. He helped found the Anti-Slavery Society in 1823 and died just before the Slavery Abolition Act was passed in 1833.

BREAKERS: A LANCASHIRE
LOVE STORY, 1779

Machine
Breakers

'Oh, John, my dearest, I hate my work as much as I do love you!' Mary Worsthorn leaned her thin, pale face against her lover's shoulder and let out a sigh as sad as the night wind off the fells.

The sound stirred John's kind heart, filling it with a fiery fusion of pity and anger. 'Ah, it's not right, my dearest Mary,' he muttered, folding his great right arm tighter about her bony shoulders. 'It's just not right you working like an Israelite in Egypt in that great mill, day on day, week on week, with never a peep of the sunshine, never setting your pretty foot on the green dales outside them narrow windows. You weren't made for that, my lovely girl! It's slavery, you know. Pure slavery!'

Mary smiled. 'I never knew you had such poetry in you, John Parker,' she laughed. 'I thought you carpenters were the silent type.'

'Not when we're roused, Mary. Any road, there was one carpenter as knew how to speak fine, wasn't there?'

'Aye, there was. Long ago.'

'Things were better long ago,' suggested John, looking through the misty rain at the lights still burning yellow in Birkacre Mill. 'Weren't no mills like Mr Arkwright's to steal away our souls.'

'He ain't stolen yours, John. Nor mine. Besides, I get good money.'

'Maybe. Depends what you call good. Ain't good if it wears you to a ghost.'

'I mean it keeps me, John, as you well know. And my old grandma, and little Peter and Will and Dotty. Tell me, where'd they be without me and Mr Arkwright's mill?'

John said nothing. They had been over this ground a thousand times and on each occasion he knew there was something wrong but could not put it into words.

'It's mill's money as keeps them out of the workhouse, my love,' added Mary.

'Only 'cos your mama and papa is no more! That were mill's doing, plain as grain.'

Mary lifted her white face towards her betrothed. 'No more, please, my dearest. You know it pains me so.'

John bent forward and kissed her on the forehead. 'Very well. No more, my poor Mary.'

She was right, he thought. There was no point in raking old ground. What's done was done . . . and yet, and yet . . . John could not get it out of his head that the mill, the new, vast mill that loomed over the vale like the castle of a conquering lord, had much to answer for.

Both Mary's parents had found work there as soon as it opened, her father as an engineer on the huge iron water wheels and her mother on the spinning machines above. Annie Worsthorn, mother of four living children and three dead, herself perished of the fever six months after the mill's opening. John said it was the mill that did it, poisoning the air. When Mary pointed out that of the eight people from the village who had died, only two had been mill workers, he merely frowned and said it didn't figure.

Joseph Worsthorn, beside himself with grief at his wife's death, had taken to the drink. Working on the great wheel late one December afternoon, he had slipped and disappeared beneath the churning metal paddles, each as big and sharp as a spade. When they found his body the next day, two miles downstream, the face was quite torn away. His eldest daughter had identified him only from the tattered remnants of his clothing.

John Parker, wheelwright and general carpenter of the nearby parish of Wheelton, had become engaged to marry Mary Worsthorn, then aged seventeen, a good year before these terrible events. John had then been out of his apprenticeship only a short while and they both knew it would be another three years at least before he had saved enough for them to marry. Now, with Mary's wages from the cotton mill all that kept her family from the disgrace and misery of the workhouse, those three years had grown to five, maybe eight.

Dotty was still only ten and it would be a good many years before she would be able to take over from her elder sister as the family's bread earner. Until then, Mary had to set aside the sweet dream of marriage to her carpenter and instead work all the hours she could.

It had stopped raining and a thin sliver of moon gleamed between the rushing clouds. John looked down at Mary's wan face. Aye, she was still as lovely as ever. But she was tired. Beneath her green eyes hung circles as dark as the blue-grey bricks of the mill's footings. Even the colouring of that cursed place is getting into her! he thought. How I hate it! It's a huge coffin, a monster that sucks the very life from all who enter!

Mary, who had been watching John's face keenly, shook her head. 'I know what you're thinking, John Parker! And you mustn't! We must be patient, and when we marry we'll be all the better for it!'

'When we marry!' said John longingly. 'When, when, when!' Moving back a little but still holding Mary's hand tightly, he took a deep breath and, very softly, began to sing, '*Lavender's blue, Mary-Mary, lavender's green, When I am king, Mary-Mary, you shall be queen!*'

'Silly boy!' laughed Mary, pleased that his mood had lightened.

'*Who told you so, Johnny-Johnny?*' she sang back, '*Who told you so? 'Twas my own heart, Johnny-Johnny, that told me so!*'

Then, standing together in the cold moonlight beside the bridge, they sang quietly together:

'*Call up your friends, Johnny-Mary, set them to work,*
Some to the plough, Johnny-Mary, some to the cart,
Some to make hay, Johnny-Mary, some to thresh corn,
Whilst you and I, Johnny-Mary, keep ourselves warm!'

It was their song, their dream, and since their engagement they had sung it at every Sunday meeting. As long as they sang together, Mary said, their love would never die.

Later that evening, walking home along the rutted road that ran between Chorley and Wheelton, John went over the evening's conversation time and again. There was no way out! He was trapped, doomed to wait years and years before he could marry. And what if, in the meantime, Mary met some other young fellow in the mill, a suitor who lived in Chorley? If she married someone like that, she'd be able to go on working at the mill, at least until she had a child. It wasn't right and it wasn't fair!

That night John Parker went to bed in a very dark mood indeed.

By chance, on Monday morning John set about repairing a broken spinning wheel. In the past such work was common and Old Grimmalt, under whom he had served his apprenticeship, had turned out twenty or thirty new wheels each year. Then, quite suddenly, the demand for wheels had almost stopped and all John now received was requests to repair old ones. The reason was obvious. Who could make a living by spinning cotton at home when it could be spun in the mill, yard after yard, spindle after spindle, one hundred times quicker and at half the price?

It's that mill again! thought John as he carefully turned a new wooden spoke on his lathe. It took away Mary's parents, it's eating away at Mary herself and it's even taking away my work. What an evil place it is!

Shortly after noon on Friday, John was roused from his workbench by the sound of shouting in the road outside. He laid down his mallet and chisel and went to see what was happening. To his astonishment he found the narrow road filled with a crowd of men and women, mostly young, walking steadily towards Chorley.

John stopped one of the throng and asked where they were from.

'Blackburn folk all!' came the reply. 'And full of anger, too!'

'Why? What's been done to you?'

'Done? We are all starving, that's what's been done! We were a spinning town afore they built that cursed mill over Chorley—'

'You mean Birkacre Mill?'

'Aye, that's the one! Taken our labour, it has. Made paupers of us all. We want it closed – closed right away, or else!' The man raised a stout stick and brandished it above his head. '*When Adam delved and Eve span*,' he yelled, 'who was then the gentleman?' All around him the crowd threw back cries of support and encouragement.

The words struck John like a bolt of lightning, firing his whole being. He was not alone! Here

28

were hundreds of people who felt about the mill as he did – and they were going to see it closed! Pausing only to grab a stick of his own and shove a loaf of bread into his coat, he locked the door and joined the crowd on the road to Chorley. Not since the day of his betrothal to Mary Worsthorn had he trodden that path with such hope in his heart.

Mary was due to work that evening. Before she set out, a neighbour, Janice Goodhew, came by and told her the mill had been closed for the weekend. Hearing that an angry mob of machine breakers was expected from Blackburn, a detachment of red-coated soldiers had been sent down from Wigan and were even now drawn up before the mill to protect it. Mary decided to use the unexpected free time to visit Martha Bagshaw, a childhood friend she had not seen for over a year. Martha, now mother of two sprightly children, had married a shepherd and lived some miles away on Anglezarke Moor. As it was a clear evening with a good moon, Mary would be able to reach Martha's that night. Making sure that her crippled grandmother and the ten-year-old Dotty were able to manage without her for a couple of nights, she left shortly before the church clock had struck six and reached her friend's cottage on the moor less than two hours later.

Before leaving, Mary had said that if she was not back when John called on Sunday, would they explain where she had gone and ask him to wait? She was surprised, therefore, not to find him at home when she returned on Sunday afternoon. He had called on Saturday, Dotty said, and on Sunday morning, too. He said he was very busy, though, and both times had left almost immediately.

'Saturday? Are you sure he came Saturday?' asked Mary, anxiety rising within her like a sickness. 'He always works Saturdays.'

'Not this one,' said Dotty, shaking her head. 'He was all hot and bothered, too. Like he had taken strong drink. Said wonderful things were going on down at the mill.'

'At the mill?' Mary's fears became more real by the second. Surely he was not with the breakers? Not her John? With a cry, she set down the basket she had been carrying and ran out of the door.

Birkacre Mill was some distance from where Mary lived. Although she knew the path as well as any, she soon realized she was not going to be able to follow it. The breakers had made rough shelters of wood and canvas on either side of the track. Sitting within, many clutching bottles and stone jars, the men leered and jeered at her menacingly. Then, as she rounded a bend between a clump of ash trees, a rough-looking fellow with bloodshot eyes lurched out and made a grab at her. She turned and ran home.

Mary busied herself with household chores for the rest of the day, trying not to think of John and what was happening at the mill. The afternoon slipped into evening, and still her betrothed had not appeared. Having waited until near midnight, she finally went to bed.

The morning dawned grey and drizzly. After Mary had handed out the last of the bread for breakfast, she went next door to ask Janice Goodhew if she had heard any news.

'Soldiers have left for Preston, so I was told,' said Janice. She was as anxious as Mary not to see the mill harmed. 'Some of the menfolk from the village have gone down to talk to the breakers, asking them not to do no damage to our livelihood.'

Mary explained how she believed her John might have joined the mob and how she had gone to look for him yesterday but had been forced to return home.

'Aye, they say they've been drinking all day and all night,' muttered Janice. 'Don't know what they're a-doing!'

'I've got to see if my John's still caught up in this,' said Mary, close to tears. 'And if he is, I must get him out. I don't know what's come over him. He's such a good, quiet man normally.'

'You like me to come with you, Mary? It'd be safer with the two of us.'

'Would you, Janice? That would be the kindest thing in all the world. I'm worried sick, you know!'

Half an hour later the two women made their way down the path towards the mill. The track was quite safe now, deserted apart from the occasional sleeping breaker snoring like a pig in his dirty bower.

A few hundred yards from their destination, the women left the path and climbed a rocky mound overlooking the valley. From the top they took stock of the scene. A small group of villagers, with a handful of soldiers dotted among them, stood some fifty paces to the left of the mill. Around the building itself the crowd of breakers surged like the tide on a rocky shore. They had clearly broken in, for the front doors had been wrenched from their hinges and lay like giant doormats before the entrance. From the inside came shouts and whoops and loud crashes.

'Oh no! No!' cried Mary. 'They're smashing the frames! It'll be weeks before they're mended and we can work again! What'll we do, Janice? What'll we do?'

Janice took her friend's hand. 'I don't know, Mary. I just don't know and— Wait! Look over there!' She pointed towards the mill. A wisp of grey smoke was drifting lazily from a top window. As they watched, it swelled to a thick black cloud with an orange heart. Within ten minutes the whole building was engulfed in fire, flames and smoke soaring angrily into the damp October air.

Standing close to Janice, Mary stared at the scene in dismay. Terrible images floated through her mind: her little brother and sisters in rags,

her grandmother dying alone on a mattress of dirty straw, herself begging in the gutter, offering anything for a crust of bread—

She was suddenly aware of a familiar voice crying her name. It was her John, rushing red-faced up the hill towards them. 'Mary! Mary!' he shouted. 'Isn't it wonderful? We've done it! It's gone! We're free!'

Reaching the top of the slope, he threw wide his arms to embrace his betrothed. His eyes were watery and his breath smelled strongly of spirits. Mary turned away.

'Mary?' he gasped. 'What is it, Mary? Don't you understand? Your prison – it's destroyed! Burned up! Gone!' He took a hesitant pace forward and tried to place a hand on Mary's shoulder.

'Take your hands off me, John Parker! You fool! Oh, why didn't you listen to me? Those breakers you joined have not destroyed my prison. They have destroyed my livelihood. It is not the mill that is burned up in those flames, John. It is our love, our life.'

Sobbing quietly, Mary took Janice's arm and walked slowly back up the muddy path towards her waiting family.

MACHINE BREAKERS

Raw cotton (like wool) is turned into cloth by being washed, combed straight and spun into threads that are woven together to make material. For thousands of years the process was done by hand. Thread-making was mostly done at home by nimble-fingered women on their spinning wheels. When, in 1769, Richard Arkwright invented a water-powered spinning machine, the livelihoods of hundreds of thousands of spinners and their families were put at risk. Arkwright's thread factory in Birkacre, Lancashire, was burned by angry 'machine breakers' in 1779. The violence was only one example of many desperate attempts to halt the industrial revolution that was changing people's lives for ever.

FREEDOM!

Queen Njinga

From all four kingdoms they came, just as the queen had requested. The people of Ndongo sent a father and son; six young hunters, travelling by night to avoid the Portuguese patrols, arrived from the six regions of Matamba; an ancient chief and his three wives represented Kongo; Tsakala the Fearless walked alone from the Jagas.

After they had eaten, Jinga rose quickly to her feet and bowed to each group in turn. All except Tsakala stood and returned the greeting.

Remaining seated, the proud chief of the Jagas responded with a simple nod of the head. Ah! thought Jinga. So that's your attitude, is it? We'll see about that!

'Great and worthy friends,' she began, looking around fiercely, 'we must fight!' Her audience muttered in approval. 'Who are these bearded men that steal our people and carry them off as slaves? They are nothing but bandits, arrogant bandits fit only for slaughter!'

One of the Matamba hunters jumped to his feet. 'Queen Jinga's right!' he exclaimed, raising his spear hand in the air. 'Let's gather our men tomorrow and drive the foreign thieves into the sea.'

'So easy to say, so difficult to do,' interrupted the Kongo chief. His three wives nodded in agreement.

'Indeed,' said the elder of the two representatives from Ndongo. 'The queen herself knows how hard it is to beat the Portuguese, with their horses and guns. Did they not drive her from her own kingdom?' He turned to face his queen. 'So what has changed, Jinga? What can you do now that you did not do last time?'

At this Tsakala the Fearless raised an eyebrow and said in a voice as deep as a cave, 'Well spoken, Salimbu. Come, Queen Jinga, tell us why you have asked us here. What do you want from us?'

Jinga stooped, lifted a spear that was lying on the ground next to her and stood clasping it like a warrior. Not much over thirty years old, she was in her prime, tall and powerful with an obvious air of majesty about her. They said that in battle she was a match for any man. Speaking in a calm and steady voice, almost as if reciting ancient lore, she declared: 'I will save you from the Portuguese.'

No one spoke.

'I will save you from the Portuguese,' she repeated just as firmly. 'That I promise.' Again, no one spoke. 'But you must give me something in return.'

'Yes?' growled Tsakala, staring hard at Jinga.

'You must give me your loyalty.'

'Meaning?'

'You must all – the Ndongo, the Matamba, the Kongo and even the Jagas – you must all accept me as your queen.'

A buzz of conversation ran around the group.

'How do we know you can defeat the Portuguese?' asked the Kongo chief.

'I have experience, I know the enemy's weakness and I have a plan. But it will not work unless we are together, with me as your leader.'

The muttering started up once more. Jinga interrupted. 'Listen, let us talk together until the sun reaches the roof of the forest. Then I will hear your decision.'

The meeting broke up into smaller groups, all talking earnestly. Only Tsakala the Fearless remained on his own. Jinga went up to him. 'Your people are proud and you are proud,' she said. 'Too proud to accept one of another tribe as queen.'

Tsakala looked up at her, thinking about what she had said. 'My people are proud,' he said eventually, 'but I am not.'

'So you could persuade them to accept me?' asked Jinga, crouching down on her haunches before him.

'Impossible!'

'Nothing's impossible for Tsakala the Fearless, surely? I'm sure you could win them over. They respect you more than anyone.'

The chief of the Jagas picked up a handful of soil and let it run through his fingers. 'Maybe I don't want to,' he said slowly.

'Maybe. But they tell me what you crave more than anything in all the world is a crested steel helmet like those worn by the Portuguese commanders.'

Tsakala looked up sharply. His eyes were shining bright.

'And an engraved sword as sharp as flint and twice as supple, from the town they call Toledo.' Tsakala did not move. 'And a pistol, with powder and bullets to shoot. They tell me you want all these things. Is it true?'

'Yes, it is. But you cannot provide them for me.'

Jinga stood up. 'I can and I will. Before ten days have passed. But only if you bring the Jagas.'

Tsakala stood and placed a hand on Jinga's arm. 'I will bring them, Queen. But if you fail and do not provide what you have promised, I will kill you.'

The leaders of the tribes met at the hour Jinga had appointed. When she asked if they would accept her as their queen, all raised their voices in approval. She thanked them, then explained what they had to do. In battle, she said, the Portuguese relied on guns and horses. To get round this, Africans had to fight at close quarters, using their nimbleness of foot and skill with clubs and spears. Conquest had made the Portuguese arrogant and impatient, Jinga continued, faults that she planned to take advantage of. Finally, her forces would have the key weapon in any battle – surprise.

For the time being Jinga would tell them no more. Under cover of darkness the meeting broke up and the leaders returned to their people to tell them what had happened and to prepare their warriors for the coming fight.

Two days later a small Portuguese patrol was set upon and all its members killed. Investigating what had happened, the local commander found spears left behind at the scene of the massacre. They all carried the tribal markings of the Matamba.

For several months now, the commander had been gathering a force for the largest slave-raiding expedition ever seen in the region. Until that moment he had not decided on a target. Now he knew. He would advance up the Jombo river, where the Matamba settlements were thickest, looting, burning, killing and enslaving as he went. By the time he returned, he swore, every man, woman and child of the Matamba would be either dead or his prisoner.

Jinga's spies had warned her of the gathering of Portuguese troops. Her idea of an attack carried out by Ndongo warriors using Matamba spears had just the effect she wanted. The Portuguese would walk into a very carefully prepared trap.

Beyond the township of Quirta, the river Jombo enters a narrow gorge. The path is strewn with sharp rocks, forcing horse riders to dismount. There is not room for more than three men to walk abreast. Above them, the walls of the ravine are covered with thick vegetation.

The Portuguese should have realized something was wrong when they found Quirta completely deserted. Not a soul was to be seen anywhere. Even the bedridden had somehow mysteriously disappeared. Furious, the commander of the slaving expedition ordered the houses to be set on fire before pressing on up the gorge.

By mid-afternoon, spread out for at least half a

mile along the narrow path, the Portuguese were decidedly fed up. As Jinga had foreseen, the riders were forced to lead their horses, and many men, exhausted by the heat, had taken off their helmets and body armour and slung them wearily over their shoulders. At the front of the column the commander looked uneasily about him. He did not like this route. It was too vulnerable, too open to ambush . . .

The first sign of attack was as silent as it was deadly. Responding to a wild bird cry, a thousand bowmen hidden in the trees launched a storm of arrows into the Portuguese ranks. Horses reared and screamed as the deadly shafts pierced their sides, necks, legs. Skewered by a dozen barbs, men were transformed into writhing hedgehogs. Amid the chaos, those who remained unharmed struggled to pull on their armour and group themselves in a defensive formation.

Before they could do so, from the slopes above poured an avalanche of frenzied warriors. War cries echoed from the rocks. A few soldiers managed to load their guns and fire, but their aim was hurried and few of the attackers were hit. Crowded together, the Portuguese stabbed in

vain at the thick leather shields forcing them back towards the river. Some stumbled and fell in, only to be speared to death by the enemy on the banks. Those who stood their ground were pummelled by heavy clubs, which broke their arms and smashed their skulls. Around them the deadly spears drove and thrust, biting through cloth and flesh until the blood flowed into the river itself and made the water run red.

At the head of the column Jinga had headed directly for the Portuguese commander. She had singled out his gleaming helmet, glittering sword and brace of bright pistols the moment he came in sight. He was just the target she needed.

Sensing her approach, the officer turned just before she reached him and lunged forward with his sword. Jinga neatly stepped to one side and drove forward with her spear. The barbed tip of the spear was deflected by the man's breastplate and cut deep into his arm. Blood spurted onto the stony ground.

As Jinga tried to draw her weapon back for a second strike, her opponent again thrust his sword forward. As before, she stepped neatly to one side. But her foot caught on a boulder and she fell, letting go of her weapon and sprawling defenceless on the ground. The commander saw his opportunity. Gritting his teeth against the pain in his arm, he lifted his sword.

The blow never fell. At the very instant the steel began to descend towards Jinga's throat, a massive club hammered into the Portuguese's side, knocking him clean off his feet. Seconds later he was dead, his neck broken by a second thunderous strike.

Jinga's saviour knelt down and removed the commander's helmet, sword and pistols.

'Tsakala,' said Jinga, rising to her feet. 'I promised to give you those.'

The chief of the Jagas turned and smiled at her. 'I know, Jinga, but I got there first.'

'So are you going to kill me, like you said?'

'Kill you? Never! Kill the finest general of our generation? The Portuguese will not return in a hurry, not after what you've done today.'

Jinga walked up to him and took his hand. 'You saved my life, Tsakala. Thank you.'

The warrior laid his hand over that of his queen. 'And you saved our people, Jinga. Thank *you*.'

ANA DE SOUSA NJINGA

Ana de Sousa Njinga, also known as Jinga, was Queen of the African kingdom of Ndongo in the early seventeenth century. The Portuguese were active in the area, gathering slaves to work on plantations in Brazil, South America. Portuguese forces drove Jinga from Ndongo in 1626. She escaped, conquered the nearby kingdom of Matamba and turned it into a centre of resistance against the slavers. In 1656 the Portuguese were finally forced to make a peace treaty with her.

I AM A COWARD

Harriet Tubman

I am not a brave man. In fact, I'm a coward. I was afraid of my mother, and if I had ever met him, I reckon I'd have been afraid of my father, too. My first nightmare was running away from snarling dogs with hot, foul breath and teeth like sharpened sugar canes. They always caught me. I still have that nightmare and now I am even more terrified of dogs than when I was young.

If I had been a little white boy, wearing shoes and going to a smart school with books under my arm each morning, then I don't suppose being a coward would have mattered very much. But this was the deep south of the USA before emancipation, and I was just a little black slave with no shoes and no schooling. I don't know what happened on other plantations, but on ours all slaves had to be the same. When it came to black people, the ideas of the owner of Brown River Plantation, Mr Herschel, were as fixed as the stars. All of them, he said, were strong but lazy, dumb-brained yet quick-tongued, and without enough imagination to understand fear. In his narrow, closed mind, no slave could ever be clever or artistic or energetic – and certainly never, ever cowardly.

To make life easy, we went along with Mr Herschel's ideas. That way we knew where we were and he thought he knew where he was. Acting lazy is easy; so is acting dumb. But how can a coward play brave? I couldn't stop myself from shaking and weeping when my mother was angry with me; I couldn't help running away when I saw a dog; when I was old enough to be sent to work in the fields, no matter how hard I tried, I couldn't hide my terror of the overseer's whip.

The overseer, Mr Tranche, was a sharp man. He knew his slaves, he said, as well as he knew his own hands. I felt him watching me, day after day, month after month, figuring me out. To confuse him, I tried a little play-acting. I stood up straight, swaggered a bit and talked loud to the other workers.

'So you think you're brave, do you, boy?' he said one evening.

I caved in straight away. 'No, sir,' I stammered. 'Just like everyone else, sir.'

Tranche's eyes narrowed. 'Just like everyone else, eh? So you ain't 'fraid of a bit of a flogging then?' He laughed and cracked his cowhide whip above my head.

The sound turned my knees to water. I fell on the ground, grovelling before his feet. 'No, sir!' I begged. 'Please don't whip me, sir! I couldn't take it, sir, I really couldn't!'

I think old Tranche was a bit surprised at first, and for a moment he just stood there. Once he'd got over what I'd done, he looked around to make sure no one else had seen me, then told me to get up. Coming up real close and sticking his whip under my chin so that my head was forced

back as far as it would go, he said, 'Right, John.
We understand each other now, don't we? You
don't want the whip, do you?'

'N-no, sir!' I stuttered.

'Then I won't give it to you – on one
condition . . .' He paused.

'Yes, sir?'

'If I need some information, John, you give
it me. Right?'

'R-right, sir!'

That's how I became a traitor.

For a long time Mr Tranche was happy with the
little bits of information I gave him. My fellow
slaves didn't like the food; about half of us believed
in God; no, I had never heard anyone speak real
bad of Mr Herschel or his overseer; and I had
certainly never heard talk of rebellion. Would I
tell him if I heard of such talk? Tranche demanded.
I replied that I would, although I hoped with
all my heart that such a moment would never
come.

Of course, it *did* come. The other young men
didn't talk to me much. They knew I was different
and didn't trust me. But after supper one evening,

as I was taking a rest under the spreading sweet gum tree behind the huts where we lived, I heard a group of them on the other side of the tree start talking in quiet voices like they didn't want anyone to hear. It was soon pretty clear why – hot talk of rising up and emancipation and freedom.

I was so frightened I feared I'd wet my pants. All those ideas were the last thing I wanted to hear, so I got up as quiet as I could and started to walk away. I hadn't got more than a few steps before a voice called my name.

'Hey, John! What're you doing?' It was Bram, the biggest mouth on the plantation.

'Nothing! Just walking!'

'Then walk this way, John.' I did as I was told. 'You hear anything?' Bram asked as I stood before him, shivering like I was one of the leaves on the sweet gum above us.

'Just the birds, Bram,' I lied.

'You sure?'

'Sure, B-Bram,' I stammered.

'Good, John,' said Bram, getting slowly to his feet and standing before me. 'Because if you ever lied to me, I'd tear you apart with my own teeth, like a dog! Now scram!'

I didn't sleep that night, or the next. Tranche noticed, of course, and asked me what the matter was. So I lied to him, too. That was it – I had now lied to Bram and Tranche. If I told the overseer about what Bram and the other boys planned, they would realize and tear me apart. But if I kept quiet and Bram caused trouble, then Tranche would see straight away that I had not passed on what I knew – and he would whip me or set the dogs on me or worse.

I wished I were dead.

Old Henry saved me. He was too old to work and spent his days pottering about the plantation doing odd jobs and chatting. Everyone seemed to like him and he was allowed to do just about anything he wanted and go any place he wanted. Clearly, Herschel and Tranche reckoned he was harmless.

They were wrong. Early one morning, about a week after I had overheard Bram's plans, Old Henry came up to me as I was washing my face by the pump and asked me what was wrong. When I said nothing, he smiled and said kindly he could spot a man in trouble five miles off. When I still wouldn't tell him my problem, he just shrugged and said casually, 'Suppose you need to get out of here . . .'

Well, I don't know what showed on my face but my heart gave such a jump I feared it'd come clean out of my chest. Oh yes, I said, the words tumbling out of my mouth like water from the pump, I would do anything to get away. With that, Old Henry told me to say nothing and leave it all to him.

Two mornings later, Old Henry came creeping up to me once more. It was all fixed, he said. Moses would lead me to safety. All I had to do was wait until Friday night, then sneak off the plantation and take the road in the direction of Church Hill. After about five miles I'd find a pile of stones on the left of the road. Nearby there was a plantation of butternut trees and in that plantation I'd find Moses. Before I could ask anything further, Old Henry had ambled off, whistling quietly to himself.

I don't know how I got to Friday. I didn't dare look at Bram or his friends and I avoided Tranche whenever I could. I was sure everyone could see in my face that I was up to something.

More than once I decided to pull out. Who was this 'Moses' anyway? Could I trust him? No, I'd stay on the plantation and . . . and . . . That was the problem. I was now three-ways terrified: of running away, of talking to Tranche and of not talking to him. In the end, running away seemed the least frightening path.

Friday evening came and I went to bed like usual. After lying there for about an hour, I sneaked out and went off towards the pit we had to use as a toilet. From there, quivering and sweating, I tiptoed off through the fields, keeping as far as possible from the house and the dogs, and made my way to the road. Then it was easy. The moon was bright and I soon made the five miles to the pile of stones.

I stopped, looked around and crept off towards the butternuts. The grove was quite thick, with a sort of clearing in the middle. On reaching this space, I stopped.

A voice cut through the darkness. 'Don't say a word!'

I jumped and peered about me. No one.

'Alone?'

'Yes, sir!'

'Name?'

'John.'

'Where from?'

'Herschel's plantation.'

After a short pause the voice said in a commanding tone, 'Turn away from me, walk forward until you find a wagon. Get into the wagon and cover yourself with timber. You have five minutes. Whatever you do, don't say a word.'

I did as I was ordered, and a short time later the wagon, with me in it, had been hitched to a horse and was rumbling along the road in goodness knows what direction. We must have travelled about six hours before we pulled off the road and stopped. On a command from my mysterious helper, I pushed the timber off me and sat up. A new day was just breaking and the air felt chill and damp. Looking towards the seat at the front of the wagon, I found a woman sitting there. She was black, like me, quite small, with high cheekbones and bright eyes that made her look handsome in a fierce kind of way.

'I'm Nancy Reeve,' she said, 'and you're my husband, Bill. We're free black folk and we're going into town to take the train. I've got the tickets. All you have to do is exactly what I tell you. If you don't, or take fright so as you might betray me, I'll shoot you dead. You got the message?'

Got it? I had no choice! I'd never met a person like this in my life before, so firm, so determined! Now I really *was* in a mess! Should I carry on with this demon or go back and . . . Well, it made me sick even to think of what happened to runaways who were recaptured. So, after changing my clothes and putting on a broad hat, on I went as Mr Reeve.

The journey into town was better than I had hoped. Nancy, as the demon had called herself, was quite friendly and we played a fun game, making up conversation like we were man and wife. I grew so relaxed that once she had to tell me to stop being cheeky. No one looked at us more than once, and by the time we were at the downtown railroad station I felt myself three-quarters along the highway to freedom.

That was mighty foolish thinking. There were police at the station, checking over the men and women going in and out. Two of them had great dogs that yelped and pulled at their chains like hell-hounds. I felt myself starting to sweat and moved to put Nancy between me and the animals.

'Frightened?' she asked, sounding a bit surprised.

I looked at her and opened my mouth, but no sound came. My throat was dry as the dust on the summer fields, so bad I couldn't even swallow. I felt tears coming into my eyes. Nancy gave me a horrified look, then took me by the arm and dragged me towards the platform for the trains heading north. There, out of sight behind some luggage, she pushed me up against the wall. 'Listen, mister,' she hissed, sticking something sharp into my stomach, 'don't you forget what I said earlier 'bout betraying me. Dead folks tell no tales.'

Shaking my head, I looked down to see what was being pushed into me. It was a gun. This woman, whoever she was, meant business. Looking back, I'm surprised I didn't die of panic there and then. But somehow – and I can't explain it – a draught of that little woman's courage flowed into me, and for the first and only time in my life I was not afraid.

We came out from behind the luggage to find ourselves face to face with a law officer, a broad fellow with a silver star on his coat and small, yellow eyes like a snake's. 'Yeah,' he drawled, real slow, 'so what have we here?'

Before I could even try to reply, Nancy cut in, 'Why, Officer, this is Bill and Nancy Reeve headed to see my folks in Virginia.'

The officer gave a scornful laugh. 'Virginia? You travelling south?'

'Sure are, Officer,' replied Nancy. I was amazed at how confident she sounded.

'Then you're even more stupid than you look,' said the officer sarcastically. 'Trains from this platform are headed north.'

Nancy gave out a little titter and turned to me. 'There, I told you, Bill! Why don't you listen to me?'

''Cos I usually know best,' I replied, trying to sound like a married man. 'I was right about the chickens, wasn't I?'

Nancy gave me the strangest look, as if to say, *Well done, actor! I never thought you had it in you!* Then she turned back to the officer and said, 'Chickens! I said all along we were on the wrong

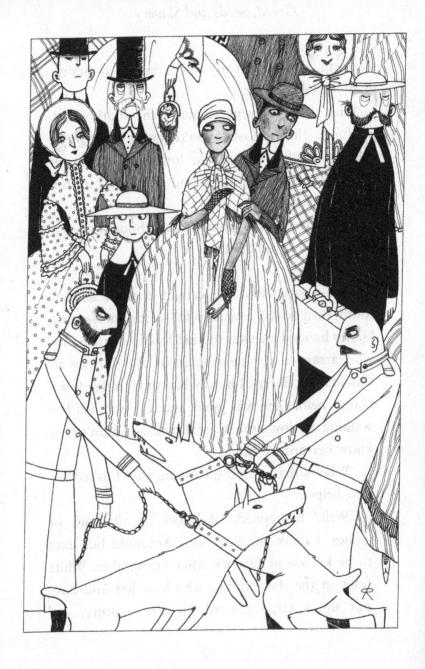

platform, Officer, but my Bill is such a stubborn man! Thank you, sir.'

With that, we went across to the southbound platform. 'Just as well you're going that way,' called the officer after us, 'otherwise I'd have taken you for runaways and had you in for questioning.'

Nancy Reeve, the women I had thought of as a demon, had saved my life.

To avoid suspicion, we caught a train headed south, then doubled back to the north. In Syracuse Nancy handed me over to kind folk in a safe house who arranged the next stage of my journey to Canada and liberty. I hardly had time to thank my Nancy before she was gone, and as I watched her walking off down the street, I realized I didn't even know her proper name.

'Who is that amazing woman, sir?' I asked my new helper.

'Well,' he replied, 'she goes by all kinds of names. I think she was born Araminta but likes to be known as Harriet, after her mother. White folks in the slave states, who hate her and have put up a large reward for her capture, call her names I wouldn't repeat in public. To the abolitionist John Brown she's the General. To folks like us she's the Stationmaster, the finest there is, on the "Underground Railroad" that carries escaped slaves like you to freedom. And passengers such as yourself call her Moses – like the Bible prophet who guided the slaves to freedom in the Promised Land.'

HARRIET TUBMAN

Araminta Ross, better known as Harriet Tubman (c.1820–1913), was born in servitude. After being badly treated, she fled to freedom and devoted the rest of her life to helping African-Americans. In the 1850s, showing remarkable efficiency, courage and determination, she helped perhaps 300 men, women and children to escape along the 'Underground Railroad'. This was a network of secret routes and safe houses by which fleeing slaves could reach Canada. After working as a spy and scout during the Civil War, she set up a home for orphaned and elderly African-Americans.

John Blanke

'You're a lucky man, John Blanke!' Wilfrid Tweedle said to me this afternoon. 'You've got everything a man could want, haven't you?'

I just laughed and said that I supposed I had. There's no point in arguing with Wilfrid about luck, not after he had one of his eyes burned out when, with his arms full of drum, he tripped over a tortoise and fell headlong into a candelabra while making music to celebrate the king's return from France. I've got both my eyes, thank God, and ears

64

and limbs and most of my teeth, so in many ways I am luckier than Wilfrid.

And yet . . .

I've made my luck. When forced to crew for Captain Wainwright on the *Andrew*, I noticed how much better musicians were treated on board ship than ordinary sailors. So I bought myself a silver whistle off a drunken fool in Cadiz and learned to play it. That wasn't luck, was it?

Then came the business with the French privateers off the coast of Madeira. Their ship was smaller than the *Andrew* but faster. Although we gave them a good run for their money, they caught us just before nightfall, coming alongside, grappling us with irons and swarming aboard like angry ants whose nest has been stirred up. We had no choice but to fight.

Fight we did, too. I saw ox-headed Daniel drive his halberd right through a man, out the other side and into the belly of the fellow behind him, then hurl them both, skewered together like sardines, into the sea. My weapon was a broad sword with a crescent-moon blade. With it I sliced and hacked away beside my shipmates until, after about half an hour of swearing and screaming, the Frenchies had been driven off our bloody decks and were hastily cutting the ropes that tied our two vessels together.

At that moment, wiping the sweat from my brow with a slippery hand, I caught sight of this half-naked, fox-faced villain sitting on the yard-arm above us. It was too late for him to climb down and rejoin his fleeing colleagues. He was trapped and had decided to make us pay the highest possible price for his death.

The rogue must have been left-handed. While holding onto the rigging with his right hand, with the other he raised an iron-tipped javelin. Horrified, I watched as he lifted the weapon high above his shoulder and took careful aim. From only fifteen feet above us he could not miss, and from the direction of his evil stare I had no doubt of his target.

Of course, it wasn't luck that I reacted as quickly as I did, although I may have been lucky in my aim. While yelling a warning at Captain Wainwright, I flung my sword towards the cowardly rascal perched above us. Round and round it whirled, whistling like the blades of the windmill on Clifton Heights in a brisk sou'wester.

The Frenchie, realizing too late what was going to happen, opened his mouth to scream. No sound came. Instead, a few seconds later, his javelin clattered harmlessly to the deck. Shortly afterwards his severed head thudded heavily down beside it and rolled awkwardly into the gunwales. That wasn't luck either, was it?

As a reward for saving his life, the captain set me ashore in Plymouth with a hearty farewell and a leather bag containing twenty guineas. 'Make good use of it, John Blanke,' he said kindly. 'Make something of yourself, for you are a man of no ordinary talents.'

I reckoned there was no living to be made cutting off French heads with whirling swords, so I hit upon the plan of making a proper musician of myself. Squeaking away on a whistle was all very well on board ship and might have earned me a few pennies in the Plymouth taverns, but I was more ambitious than that. So I spent one of the captain's guineas on the finest brass trumpet I could find. I taught myself to play and, to my delight, found that the talent God had given me for whistle-playing applied to trumpeting too. Before long I was asked to play whenever a fine band was needed – at banquets, feasts, tournaments and triumphs throughout the counties of the south-west. Luck? I think not!

It was on one of these occasions – a great gathering to honour the betrothal of Squire Russell's eldest son to the pretty but ill-tempered daughter of an Exeter merchant – that Wilfrid Tweedle, the master musician who had hired me, suggested I accompany him to London. He had a friend, he said, who would find us well-paid work there, even occasionally at court. It worked out just as Wilfrid had promised, although the court of the seventh King Henry was not quite the buzzing honeypot I had expected. That all changed, however, when his son became king.

In those days, long before he began his quarrel with the bishop of Rome and started changing his wives quicker than most men do their breeches, the eighth King Henry was a cheerful young man. He was newly married, too, and full of the joys of youth. When his queen gave birth to a son, he went mad with delight. As there was nothing he liked better than showing off his skill and strength before crowds of admiring subjects, he planned to celebrate the birth of an heir with a magnificent tournament. This suited me perfectly because tournaments required music, especially trumpets.

Nothing but the best would do, and the Master of the King's Music scoured the land for the finest trumpeters. I had already played at court, so had a head's start on most of the others. Nevertheless, I had to go through the same selection process. We were commanded to play in the gardens of Whitehall Palace before a group of officials headed by a tall, bird-like gentleman who had, appropriately enough, a long wavy ostrich feather in his hat. After standing the ten hopefuls in a line before him, he told us that just four were required to play at the tournament. The best four.

Our instructions were simple. 'Play something grand and noble,' the ostrich ordered. 'Something that befits the entry of a mighty king into the lists.' We played where we stood, beginning when he pointed a long finger at us and stopping when he clapped his white hands.

I played last. Although nervous, after hearing the others I was confident of my ability and played what I thought was a suitably noble and stirring tune. I believe the ostrich was impressed, too, for he let me finish my piece and then smiled and made gestures of approval with his hands. My heart jumped in anticipation.

Too soon! The courtier sitting next to the ostrich, some secretary or other with watery blue eyes, shook his head and frowned. 'Great Heavens, no!' he drawled, looking at me as if I were a creature left over from before Noah's Flood. 'He'd scare the wits out of the ladies! Think of the queen, sir! Think of the queen!'

The ostrich announced the committee's choice shortly afterwards, and the rejected candidates, myself among them, packed away our instruments and prepared to be escorted from the palace. Just then there was a great scurrying and scuffling along the path to our left. A bevy of elegant ladies appeared, dressed in the most exquisite finery I had ever seen. Instinctively, we all removed our hats and bowed.

The lady at the centre of the group, a little shorter than the others but clearly the most

distinguished, smiled at the ostrich and said in a pretty foreign accent, 'These are the trumpeters for the tournament? I am hearing them – very good playing!'

The ostrich bowed again. 'I am so glad you like our music, Your Highness. But not all these men will be playing for us. Only the four most accomplished, which I have here selected.' He gestured towards the chosen trumpeters.

The queen – for the graceful lady was indeed none other than Her Royal Highness Queen Catherine, from the Spanish kingdom of Aragon – clapped her hands and said with a little laugh, 'Excellent! My ladies and I made also our choice while we are listening. We are all agreeing that one is the best.'

The ostrich looked slightly uncomfortable. 'Indeed, Your Highness. And if I may ask, which was that?'

'Come, come! Who else but he who played last? So passionate, so delicate, so powerful . . .'

That is how I, John Blanke, the black trumpeter, came to play in the great tournament before Their Highnesses and all the nobility of the realm. It was the start of a fine career. My playing is still much admired and I have remained a favourite at court for many years.

So Wilfrid calls me a lucky man. Maybe. But was it luck that I taught myself the whistle, saved the life of Captain Wainwright and became the finest trumpeter in the land? Was it luck that, as Her Highness recognized, I played better than the others that morning at Whitehall Palace? No, it was talent, determination and sheer hard work.

As far as real luck was concerned, mine ran out twenty-four years ago, when I was just eleven years old. One bright morning I was seized, dragged from my home and sold as a slave to a Portuguese merchant, who swapped me with Captain Wainwright for a bale of wool and two German pistols. Since then I have lived alone. Without mother, father, brothers, sisters or any other family, I am an alien in a foreign land. Wilfrid said I have everything a man could want. Really? He may have lost his eye, but I have lost all that was dearest to my heart.

I know full well which is the luckier man.

TRUMPETER JOHN BLANKE

Documents tell us that John Blanke (a racist joke: 'blanke' meant 'white'), 'the blacke trumpeter', played for Henry VII and Henry VIII, and he is pictured performing at a great tournament of 1511. We do not know how John came to England. The Portuguese began shipping African slaves to Europe in 1441, so the Tudor trumpeter may well have been a Portuguese slave who had gained his freedom.

Annie Burton

I was born around 1858 – a slave girl to a
slave mother in an American slave state. They
said my father was a free man. Mrs Eustasia
Campbell, my mistress, reckoned he was
an Englishman from Liverpool who owned a
plantation next to ours. I never knew him, though
I saw him once or twice when I was about four
years old, riding all high and mighty in his gig.
My mistress once hailed him and asked why
he didn't stop and speak to his darling Annie, but
he just stared ahead and continued on his way.

That's how it was in those days. I can hear you saying, 'Why, that's terrible, Annie! You must've been so unhappy!' But to tell you the truth, I wasn't unhappy. At least, I don't remember being so. Time is like those muslin filters they used on the cows' milk – it takes out the bad bits and leaves mostly only the sweetness.

I recall much sweetness. We were carefree, barefoot children, fourteen black and ten white, all playing together on our plantation in the southern sunshine. We didn't get supper and only a little piece of bread in the morning, yet I don't think we went hungry. Midday meal times were a greedy gathering around a great wooden bowl, scooping and scraping with our oyster-shell spoons at whatever had been cooked up for us. Better than all that was the thieving.

We were terrible sinners! Nothing in the fields was safe from our wicked little fingers – corn cobs, sweet potatoes, sugar cane, peanuts, we carried them all off for private feasts under the trees beyond the cotton fields. And I believe the adults never knew it was us! They said it was the crows or the fairies. We also ate the food we carried to the workers in the fields at midday, but that was more dangerous. If we thieved too much, which we normally did, then they complained when they got home and we were whipped.

That brings me to whipping. When I look back now, I see it was wrong, mighty wrong. But in those days we didn't know any better. We accepted it – most of us, at least – as the rough part of plantation life. We children were whipped with canes; twenty strokes, it might be for stealing. It hurt and made us howl enough to wake the dead and raised great welts on our backs and buttocks so as we couldn't sit down for days; but we got over it and went on stealing just the same. It was different for adults.

An adult whipping was a big thing. It was carried out by the white overseer at the whipping post outside the great barn. All workers, slave and others, had to watch. The offender was tied to the post with ropes, their hands round the other side, coils binding their feet to stop them jumping about. The overseer, Mr Grindal, read out the offence and straight away picked up a great bullhide whip of the kind used to drive cattle. After he had cracked it in the air a few times to get his arm a-loose, he brought it down across the back of the victim with a mighty swish and slap. The person being whipped then let out some sort of cry or groan before the second blow.

This swishing and hollering and weeping went on until the punishment was over. Sometimes the whip broke the skin and the offender was left all bruised and bloodied, as if someone had painted red lines over their body with a brush. I saw one old man collapse in a heap when his ropes were cut. He never got up again, either. Died right there and then. They say he had a weak heart and the shock of the whipping caused it to bust in two.

Mother was whipped. Just the once, but that was enough.

My mother and my mistress, Mrs Eustasia, had been children together on the plantation. They had grown up just like we all did, playing together, stealing peanuts together and generally having a good time. When they were older, they were mothers together, too. They remained close, except that the mistress had married Mr Campbell, who owned the whole plantation, while Mother had married no one and was just a household slave.

One day, as we were playing in the yard, we heard a terrible shouting and cursing in the house.

It seems the mistress had accused Mother of doing something wrong, and she said she hadn't done it, and now the two of them were hammering away like a pair of spitting tomcats. Mother being a slave, there was only one outcome possible. The mistress said she had to be whipped, which was something no one had ever dared do to Mother before.

It wasn't a real savage flogging, just a few strokes at the post and then it was over. But even that was too much for Mother. Her pride had been dented like it had been run over by a whole team of horses. Her eyes flashed fire, her nostrils flared wide and she breathed so deep I thought she would burst with all the air she took in.

'That's it!' she declared. 'I ain't no criminal and I ain't going to be treated like one.' She was a proud lady, my mother, and the mistress found it out too late. When we awoke the next morning, we were orphans. Mother had run away during the night and we didn't know as we would ever see her again.

There were three of us orphan children: Caroline, the eldest, myself and little Henry. We hadn't known a family like you read about in books. There were lots of adults in our lives – Mother and the master and the mistress being the most important ones. So when Mother went away, we were sad for a while, then bobbed up again like ducks on a pond. I think that's what slavery does to you – it takes away the little things that make you feel yourself. When you're a slave, you aren't really a person so you don't get a chance to grow the sentiments most normal folks have. Just as I had never known no daddy, so now I got used to having no mother, and it didn't make me specially sad – not after a month or two anyway.

Life as orphans went on as before and the mistress treated us pretty much like she did her own children, which wasn't too bad. Then war broke out and we were told of soldiers and armies moving around the South and how the Yankees from the North were the bad ones. Finally the day came when President Lincoln signed the piece of paper – the Emancipation Proclamation, it was called – that set all the slaves free by the law of the United States of America. The mistress wanted to keep it a secret but the master said everybody would find out soon enough so he told his workers right away.

All the slaves, except those who were too feeble or sickly, left the plantation the moment they heard the news. But not Caroline, Henry and me. We had nowhere to go and the mistress wanted to keep us. We were useful to her and I reckon she was pretty fond of us, too. It pains me to say it, but I'm not sure we wanted to go anywhere ourselves, either. For a little time, seeing as we were the only help around the whole plantation, we were important.

Mother came back for us at the end of the year, marching up to the house like she owned it and facing up to the mistress and saying she wanted her children back there and then. The mistress called her all sorts of names I won't repeat and told her to go away.

'You're abducting my children, Mrs Campbell,' said Mother, like the two of them had never been friends, 'and that's against the law.'

'And you abandoned your children like you never wanted them,' replied the mistress. 'Why, it's been a good nine months since that damned proclamation and only now you decide you want them back. Is that a true mother?'

'Truer than you,' shouted Mother, with one of her angers coming on fast. 'You've stolen them! Slaver!'

They went on yelling like this until the mistress threatened to set the dogs on Mother and she had to back off down to the gate. We didn't know what to make of it all. I was frightened of them both. But Caroline, being almost grown up by now, declared that Mother was in the right and we should be with her.

About supper time Caroline sneaked down to the gate and talked to Mother, who was hiding in some trees nearby. Then our big sister came back and collected Henry and me and led the three of us to the gate. With tears in her eyes, Mother picked up Henry, and Caroline put me on her shoulders and we all three set off across the fields to a little cabin Mother had taken. I was so confused and tired and happy and sad, all at the same time, that I didn't speak one word but sat there on the dirt floor like a dumb child.

A bit later, the mistress's sons came riding up on their horses and demanded Mother hand us over to them. She refused.

'Tell me, boys,' she said, sounding as high as a

judge, 'is it correct there's a Yankee general nearby that can tell us the rights and wrongs of what you ask? Shall we go over and ask his advice?'

On hearing this, the men rode off and left us in peace.

I never saw the mistress or the plantation ever again, though I thought much about them and still do. You see, though there's not one little chip of good in slavery, there is good in almost all folk. Getting rid of bad customs is fine and necessary, but in the end it's still people that matter most.

ANNIE L. BURTON
For 250 years the farming economy of the southern United States was based on slavery. The cotton industry, it was said, depended on it. Slavery was finally abolished after the defeat of the South in the Civil War (1861–5), although discrimination against African-Americans remained strong for at least another century. This story is based on Annie Burton's Memories of Childhood's Slavery Days *(1909), a fascinating account of her life as a slave in the Old South.*

King Darius I

General Maziar's eyes narrowed to bright crevices in his weather-beaten face. 'She will be mine, of course! I have priority.'

'Oh yes?' General Farid did not like Maziar's confidence. It made him suspect that his rival knew something he did not. 'And what sort of priority is that, pray?'

'In the last two battles His Majesty gave me command of the right wing, the senior flank.' Maziar's skin folded like an empty water bottle as he allowed himself a rare smile. 'The senior commander always has priority in His Majesty's favours. The girl's as good as mine, Farid. Just give up!'

Farid was not the sort of man to give up, certainly not without a fight. He was younger than Maziar, for sure, but he reckoned he was just as talented. Hadn't he been given command of the leading force when the Persian troops had swept down into the Indus valley? Wasn't it his plan for crossing the Nari river that King Darius had adopted? But the strongest argument of all for granting him the hand of Princess Amala in marriage was that he loved her.

From the moment Farid had first set eyes on the lovely Indian princess, he had been obsessed with her. He dreamed of her, he made feeble excuses to pass by her tent in the hope of catching sight of her, and he even composed poems in her honour (in secret, of course). If King Darius gave permission for anyone but himself to marry the gracious Amala, Farid really did believe he would die of a broken heart.

'You forget one thing, Maziar,' said Farid quickly, trying hard to control his emotions.

'Princess Amala would not accept you.'

Maziar snorted. 'Rubbish! Haven't you seen the looks she gives me? Pure adoration!'

'Adoration? What in the name of holy Zarthosht are you talking about? Only the other day she said to me—'

'You've spoken with her? Don't lie!' It was Maziar's turn to be worried. Instinctively he clenched his huge fists, driving his broken nails into the palms.

Unnoticed by the squabbling generals, a distinguished-looking figure in a turquoise and scarlet robe emerged from the shadows of the royal tent and stood watching them keenly.

Farid's face flushed with anger. 'Are you calling me a liar, Maziar?'

'Maybe. You haven't talked to her!'

'I have, fool!'

Maziar felt for his sword. 'Take that back, Farid!'

'Why should I? You called me a liar!' Farid's hand moved to the blade hanging at his side.

'And you are a liar!'

'Right, Maziar—'

A cool voice cut across the evening air.

'Maziar! Farid! Gentlemen! Is this the way for our commanders to behave? Is this an example to set your men? Above all, is this how you want your king to see you? Because if you do, he is not impressed!'

The two generals stood stock-still, their heads bowed.

'Speak!'

Farid raised his eyes a little. 'I am very sorry, Your Majesty. I did not realize—'

'You did not realize we were watching? So if we had not been dragged outside by the fearful racket you were making, you would have carried on?'

'No, sire. Of course not!'

'Huh!' King Darius took a couple of steps forward. 'So why in the name of the Wise Lord were you about to cut each other to pieces?'

Between them, greatly embarrassed, the men explained their quarrel. After arriving in the Indus valley from the Khyber Pass, Darius had scattered the armies of the Indian king in two fierce battles. To secure a lasting peace, he had suggested that Princess Amala, the twenty-year-old daughter of the defeated king, might like to marry a Persian nobleman. To help her father, the lady had agreed

– as long as she could find a suitable groom.

Maziar and Farid had immediately sought the honour of her hand, but so far Amala had made no public demonstration of her preference. In private, though, she knew very well whom she wanted. Maziar, dignified, brave and honest, was just not her type. Besides, he was at least twenty years older than her and had been married twice before. Farid, on the other hand, was far more to her liking. His lively face, quick movements and sleek black hair caught her eye the moment she arrived in the Persian camp. More importantly, as the younger general had told Maziar, he had managed to talk to her once or twice in private. He made her laugh and the moment he had to go, she longed for him to return. Yes, in her heart Princess Amala knew full well whom she wished to marry.

Amala also knew it was not that simple. For royalty, marriage never is. Her father and most of his advisers wanted her to marry Maziar, the senior, richer and more powerful man. She thought that was what King Darius had in mind, too. That is why, when the king sent for her and asked her to settle the quarrel between his generals there and then by choosing one of them as a husband, she looked at each in turn before saying quietly, 'O King, I do not know these men well enough. I cannot choose now.'

'Very well,' said Darius, growing tired of the whole business. 'We will arrange for them to show you their qualities. A good husband needs skill, strength and sophistication, do you agree?'

Princess Amala nodded.

'Then we will have a contest between Maziar and Farid to show their skill, strength and sophistication. Will you accept the winner as your husband?'

Amala felt she had no choice but to agree. 'I will,' she said, giving Farid a glance she hoped he understood as wishing him luck.

'Right. This is the contest,' went on Darius. 'First, to test their skill, each man will shoot six arrows at a pole fifty paces distant. Whichever of the two pierces the pole with the most arrows is the winner. Strength we will test by lifting rocks. The man who can raise the heaviest rock above his head will be the winner. As for sophistication . . .'

The king paused a moment, running his fingers

down his well-clipped beard, before saying with a chuckle, 'We have it! Each man will prepare a feast for ourselves and fifty courtiers. The meal we enjoy most will be the winner. We will start tomorrow one hour after sunrise.'

So saying, Darius turned on his heel and retired to his tent for the night.

Farid easily won the shooting match. With a steady hand and a sharp eye, he pierced the pole four times while his rival managed only once. The situation was reversed with the rock lifting. Sweating and straining, Farid just managed to heave a piece of rock the size of a small goat high above his head before dropping it to the ground with a crash and falling over himself. Maziar sniffed the air, stepped forward, grabbed the rock and raised it above his head with one hand. Then, balancing it there, he seized a second stone similar in size to the first and lifted that into the air, too. Princess Amala, watching at a safe distance, clapped politely.

All square! The contest would be decided on sophistication – the feast. The meals were to be held on consecutive evenings, Maziar's first.

He served it outdoors on long wooden tables decorated with lotus flowers and palm leaves. Under his command, the royal cooks prepared seven glorious dishes, starting with spiced pigeon sprinkled with coriander, progressing to roast wild duck and oranges, and finishing with exotic fruits chilled with ice brought down from the mountains. Seven different wines were drunk from golden goblets.

At the end of the meal Darius sat back and looked around him. 'That was the finest meal we have ever eaten,' he said with a broad smile of contentment. 'The fruit might have been a trifle sweeter, for I adore sweetness, but everything else was perfect. Quite perfect!' He leaned across towards Amala. 'Do we really need to have a feast tomorrow, Princess? No one could prepare a meal like that! Let's say now that Maziar has won, shall we?'

Amala smiled, her perfectly white teeth gleaming in the summer moonlight. 'It was a wonderful meal indeed, o King! Yet, as you say, the fruit was a little bitter. Perhaps . . .'

Maziar, who was standing behind the king's chair, leaned forward and explained, 'There are no bees in this region, my dear lady, so there is no honey to sweeten the fruit. It was, I assure you, the sweetest in all the markets for miles around.'

'Of course, no bees,' said Amala politely. 'Even so, I believe it would be fair to give General Farid his chance. I'm sure our appetites will have returned by this time tomorrow.'

The king agreed, and the following evening the guests again sat down to enjoy a splendid feast. It was served beneath a specially built canopy of gleaming silk on tables lit with candles whose holders shone with semi-precious stones. Again there were seven dishes. The largest, which drew a round of applause from the guests, was a wild boar stuffed with peacock, stuffed with peppered duck, stuffed with cinnamon and garlic in a paste of seeds. As on the previous evening, the meal ended with ripe fruit served on silver dishes.

Darius frowned as the dishes were set down before him. 'This is supposed to be a test of sophistication, Farid. We hardly think it's sophisticated to give us the same old bitter mangoes.'

Bowing low, Farid clicked his fingers. Six serving girls instantly appeared from the kitchen

tent, each bearing a pot of golden liquid. As the first girl prepared to spoon some of it over the fruit, Darius said excitedly, 'Honey? By the great sun, Farid, you have found some honey!'

'No, sire,' replied Farid, winking towards Amala, 'it is not honey. There is no honey in this region.'

'Then what is it?'

'It is called "sahkara", sire, and it comes from a cane. If it please Your Majesty to try some, I am sure you will find it sweeter than honey.'

King Darius tasted the sugar and, indeed, it was sweeter than honey.

Overjoyed to find such delight in a land without bees, King Darius judged Farid to have won the contest and with it the hand of Princess Amala. He also ordered bundles of sahkara canes to be transported back to Persia. Later, when Amala confessed that, to win the man she loved, she had sneaked into Farid's kitchens and told him where to find the secret sahkara, the king forgave her at once. 'How could we ever be angry,' he said, 'with one who has brought such sweetness into our world?'

DARIUS I

Darius I was King of Persia between 548 and 486 BC. He expanded and reorganized the Persian Empire, making it one of the best-governed in the world. It was he, they say, who introduced sugar cane to the Middle East, from where it became available in Europe. When the Persians first came across it, the 'reed which gives honey without bees' caused surprise as well as delight.

THE OPENING

François Toussaint

The three slaves nodded in agreement, their heads slowly rising and falling like the beam of the new pumping engine installed down by the river.

'Yep,' said Jacob, gazing out over the rolling green fields of the plantation, 'there was no one to match him. My hero, first to last!'

'Mine, too,' added Abraham, the youngest of the group.

'Least we're agreed on something,' concluded

Zak. He folded his strong arms and leaned back against the smooth bark of the buttonwood beneath which the three men had sat since after breakfast, enjoying their day of rest. However hard Mr Trudeau might drive them the rest of the week, he was a man of faith and would never make his slaves work on Sundays.

Abraham took out a tobacco leaf, pulled off a strip and began to chew it. 'Strange name, though,' he said after a while.

Jacob looked at him sideways. 'What is?'

'"Toussaint L'Ouverture". It's not like yours, Jacob, or mine. I mean, it's not from the Bible.'

'Is sort of,' Jacob explained. 'The first bit, any road. "Toussaint" means "All Saints" in French. Most probably he was born on the day of All Saints.'

'That figures. He was a kind of soldier and saint mixed together, wasn't he?'

'Suppose so.'

'What about the "L'Ouverture" bit? I don't recall no "L'Ouverture" in the Bible, lest he was someone we don't remember in those lists of begats.'

'Not from the Bible, boys,' interrupted Zak,

who had now closed his eyes and looked pretty much asleep.

Abraham leaned forward and put his elbows on his knees. 'Come on, Zak! You were one of his soldiers in the days of freedom. Where'd it come from? How'd he get to be called "L'Ouverture"?'

Zak opened his eyes a fraction. 'You really want to know?'

'Sure do,' said Jacob. 'And since you're the only one as knows, you gotta tell us. No point in having the man as a hero if we don't know where his name comes from.'

'Is that so?' retorted Zak, opening his eyes a bit wider and giving Jacob a quizzical look. 'Very well then. Make yourselves easy and I'll tell you how that great man, Mr Toussaint, came also to be known as L'Ouverture.

'There are three things you need to know about Mr François Dominique Toussaint – that was the full name his mammy and pappy gave him when he was baptized into the Holy Catholic Church. The first thing is that he didn't rest one short minute longer than he had to. I never seen a man like it. He was up before the birds and never went

to sleep till the fruit bats had been flapping about the trees for a good three hours. You know, I once saw him stop a letter he was writing, run up a hill a good two mile away, climb a tree at the top to spy out the land, shin down again, run back to his letter and carry on writing as if he'd never been away. He was like the sea, always moving. Made you tired just to look at him.

'The second thing was Mr Toussaint's brain. I reckon he had two of them packed into that skull of his, one for remembering and the other for thinking. He never forgot a name and he could work out problems like a lightning strike – flash! He had the answer!

'Now I've heard it told that great men are often like Mr Toussaint, mighty fast of acting and thinking, but that they usually go rotten inside. They get all full of themselves and come to believe they're kings or gods or whatever. Not Mr Toussaint. No way.

'That man never forgot where he'd come from nor where he was going. They wanted to make him king once, you know that? King of Haiti. When he heard of the plan, he looked like a barrel of gunpowder with a fuse burning on the top. "King!" he shouts. "I'm a man come to help the African people. You make me a king and we'll be just like our enemies, raising people up above their fellows for no reason. Jesus Christ is my king and I ain't having no other. No, sir, the title 'L'Ouverture' is good enough for me. I've no room for any more."

'There you are, that gives you some measure of the man.

'It all began when we heard that back in France the people had risen up in the name of liberty, equality and brotherhood. It was what they called a revolution. Mutterings began among the slaves: if the French could have a revolution, why not us? A revolt began in the north and soon spread to other areas. There never was such a killing! Men, women, boys, girls, servants – they slew anyone they could get hold of who was white or who worked for them. I remember little children, innocent as innocent, hanging by their necks from the trees while birds pecked at their dead eyes. It was a good time and a bad time all mixed up.

'It didn't last, though. The French soon got themselves organized and brought in more soldiers to put down the revolt. The tide turned and it was we Africans who were slaughtered. We had no leadership, you see. The men who had put themselves at the head of the rebels were no good – vain as ladies and brains like leaky buckets. They did not know how to organize their men. There was no discipline.

'That's not quite true. One of our leaders knew how to organize; how to give his men discipline. That was the man you were talking about, Mr Toussaint. He had been educated and knew how to read and write like a gentleman. The men under his command did not run about wildly like the other rebels, getting silly with drinking and singing songs all night so they were not able to fight in the morning. No, Mr Toussaint's soldiers obeyed orders. If they did not, they were punished. Soon, his was the only rebel force left and I was proud to be part of it.

'Mr Toussaint had read about fighting, about how great generals had defeated armies stronger than theirs. "It's all a matter of the right strategy and tactics, Zak," he said to me when I asked him why he was not defeated. I don't know what those two things are but I'm sure he was right.

Instead of rushing into fights like the others had done, we waited. We waited for more men to join us in the hills; then we waited still longer while Mr Toussaint taught them how to be soldiers. Training, he called it.

'When our commander reckoned we were ready, we had a small battle. Spies told us a band of French soldiers was camped in the valley below our hideout. Mr Toussaint made a plan and ordered that we had to follow it whatever happened during the fight. It wasn't easy, but we managed it. One of our "regiments", as Mr Toussaint had named the groups we were divided into, attacked the enemy at dawn and drove them from their camp. Our other two regiments now came out of their hidden positions and chopped the runaways down like sugar cane as they tried to escape. Not one survived, not even their commander.

'That gave us confidence and we won more little victories. We grew more bold, until one evening Toussaint called his officers together and said it was time for what he called the "decisive blow". A large French force was moving along the plain to the east of Cap-Haïtien. For the first time we would face them head-on, on the battlefield. They say our commander's eyes shone like jewels as he explained what we had to do. This was the test of whether we were a real army or just an angry mob. We had the spirit, the fire in our bellies, but we also had to remember the discipline. If we fell into disorder, he warned, we would be chopped to pieces like firewood.

'We lined up on the plain in our three regiments. General – no longer "Mr" – Toussaint commanded the centre, which is where I was. Charles Dupré commanded the left and Georges Millard the right. All three had been household slaves so had some education. As soon as they saw us coming, the French got into position with a great blaring of trumpets and clattering of drums. I was so excited I couldn't stop my gun from shaking in my hand. My friend Abel, standing next to me, was quietly saying his prayers.

'About noon, with more clattering of drums, the French began advancing towards us. Following his orders, Dupré led his men towards them then veered off to the left. Just as General Toussaint had said they would, the enemy followed. Next Millard and his men went forward, trying to get round the right side of the troops in front of him. Seeing this, the French edged over to stop them. Again, it was just as our commander had predicted.

'By now the leading soldiers of both sides had met and the sounds of battle – gunshots, cries, the neighing of horses, clashes of steel – floated over the plain towards where we stood. We had not budged one inch. Suddenly a trumpet blared behind us. It was the signal to charge! With men on horseback on either side to protect us, we advanced on the French centre.

'Thanks to General Toussaint's brilliant plan, the French force had been dragged left and right, leaving a gap in the middle of their line. It was for this opening that we ran. Too late the French commander realized his mistake and sent a few horsemen to meet us. These were easily brushed aside and within ten minutes we had passed clean though the enemy ranks and were turning to attack them from behind. We had them surrounded.

'The battle lasted no more than an hour. Many French dropped their guns and ran for the woods. A good many were cut down by our cavalry before they got there. The rest fought on, some bravely, others tying white handkerchiefs to their swords and waving them in the air as a sign that they had surrendered. I didn't see much action myself. I stabbed one man in the eye and watched, fascinated, as he clasped his hands over the wound to stop the blood gushing out. Someone else more or less finished him off with a thrust through the belly. After that, I shouted a lot but did no more than hack at an elderly-looking Frenchman who was trying to get away. I missed his body but managed to slice off part of his elbow. The bone gleamed white in the sunlight.

'When it was clear we had won a great victory, we gathered round our general and hollered and cheered like madmen. He sat there on his horse, smiling and raising his hat. After a while he lifted his hand to signal that he wished to speak. Immediately we all fell silent.

'General Toussaint began by thanking us and praising our courage. He thanked God, too, for the victory of right over wrong. Discipline, he said, had been the key. We had kept our discipline when the enemy had lost theirs. "They split," he shouted, "like a hewn tree. You were the axe. They left an opening in their centre and you went through it. Through the opening to victory!

'"That opening was more than just a way to

triumph, men. It was a symbol. Here today we have made a wider opening, a passageway through which I pray all slaves will soon walk to freedom!"

'I think we were still cheering when the sun went down and a silver moon rose over the bloody field.'

Zak leaned back against the tree. 'And that, Jacob and Abraham, is how General Toussaint L'Ouverture got his name. L'ouverture, you see, is the French for "opening".'

Abraham rubbed his hands over his face. 'Some hero, Zak,' he mused. 'You must be mighty proud to have known him. But that opening to freedom he spoke of – well, it got closed up pretty soon. Here we all are back as slaves again.'

Zak closed his eyes. 'Opening's still there, boy. And we'll get there soon enough, just as General Toussaint-L'Ouverture promised. Just you wait and see.'

TOUSSAINT L'OUVERTURE

François Dominique Toussaint (c.1743–1803), later known as Toussaint L'Ouverture, was an educated slave in the French colony of Saint Dominigue (Haiti).

Inspired by the ideas of the French Revolution, he led a successful revolt which won freedom for the slaves and independence for their territory. Emperor Napoleon I, a racist and supporter of slavery, refused to accept what had happened. In 1802, his army re-conquered Saint Dominigue. Toussaint L'Ouverture was betrayed and shipped to France, where he died under interrogation.

THE SACRIFICE

The Treatment
of Slaves

Abu Sebba carefully guided his dhow round the headland and pointed its prow towards the narrow opening between the towers that guarded the harbour entrance.

'Seems you know the approach pretty well, Captain,' said Abdullah, the mate. 'Sure you haven't been here before?'

Abu Sebba shook his head. Glancing keenly around him, he replied firmly, 'Never. I don't know anything about the place, Abdullah.' He

made a mental note to ask Allah's forgiveness
for having lied. Changing the subject, he asked,
'What's that hanging on the towers? Some sort
of charm?'

Abdullah snorted. 'Charm! You could say that,
Captain. It's all that's left of a skeleton.'

Abu Sebba screwed up his eyes against the glare
and examined the bleached bones more carefully.
'Human?'

'Aye, poor old devil!'

'What had he done to be strung up there?'

Abdullah breathed in deeply through his nose
in a gesture of silent disapproval. 'They say he
helped a slave to escape. You know better than I
do, Captain, what Arabs are like with something
they've paid for – be it object, be it human, they
hate to lose it, don't they?'

Abu Sebba had stopped listening. He knew
all too well what the mate was talking about. All
too well . . .

Twenty-eight years previously, Abu Sebba – or
Usama, as he was then – had been one of fifteen
slave boys bought by a prosperous Arab merchant,
Ibn Massoud. The captives were Africans taken

111

from a large village two weeks' journey inland from Mozambique. The merchant didn't need fifteen boys and he didn't want fifteen boys, but he knew that the chances of more than two surviving what lay ahead were pretty slight, so he took the lot. Bargain price.

For some six months, under the watchful eye of Old Mahmood, the slave who had served Ibn Massoud for over thirty years, the boys were well cared for and enjoyed an easy-going existence. They were not allowed outside the family compound, of course, but otherwise they were free to do almost as they pleased.

This carefree existence came to a sudden end one Friday in May. After morning prayers Lubabah, the newest and prettiest of the merchant's eleven wives, complained to her husband that one of the young slaves had been trying to peep over the wall into the garden of the harem. At once Ibn Massoud ordered the 'process' to begin.

The next morning Old Mahmood reluctantly took aside the offender and two of his friends and led them to the household's large kitchen. As the door shut behind them, Usama caught a glimpse

of an old man with a long white beard dressed in a dirty brown robe. He was surrounded by several powerful-looking men and in his right hand he held a curious-looking curved knife.

A minute or so later, the peace of the courtyard was shattered by the most terrible noises Usama had ever heard in all his short life. First came a pitiful begging and sobbing. It was soon followed by hideous screams, worse by far than those made by pigs having their throats cut. The sounds echoed on and on, tearing the air with a ghastly cacophony of pain and wretchedness, until it seemed that the terrible din would crack the very walls of the kitchen. Standing outside, the rest of the boys watched in horror as a trickle of blood escaped under the kitchen door and dried dark in the spring sunshine.

That afternoon, three more boys were taken into the kitchen, this time kicking and yelling for mercy. Again the sounds of torture set their friends outside howling in sympathy, fear and despair. Throughout it all, Old Mahmood sat staring motionless. When asked what was going on, he replied simply that it was the 'process' all slaves had to endure. Had it been done to him then? Indeed it had. And was it necessary to go through it to become a man? No, quite the opposite. When pressed to say more, Mahmood shook his head and walked slowly away.

Usama did not sleep that night. None of the boys who had disappeared into the kitchen had returned and he could not get the awful noise of their torment out of his head. Eventually, driven to the edge of despair by worry, he rose from his thin mattress and tiptoed over to Old Mahmood's bed in the corner of the dormitory.

'Yes, little one?' the old slave asked as the boy knelt silently at his bedside.

'You are awake, too, Uncle?' whispered Usama in surprise. Because of his gentle, almost fatherly manner, the boys had called Mahmood 'Uncle' from the day of their arrival.

'Of course! Who can find peace on a night like this?'

'You mean, you mean . . . ?' Usama tried not to cry.

'Yes, I feel it as you do, little one.' Mahmood stretched out a hand and ruffled the boy's curly hair.

The kindness was more than Usama could bear. His heart burst, and with tears streaming down his face he cried, 'Oh please, Uncle, what is this "process"? Why are they being so cruel? What wrong have we done? I don't want it, Uncle! I really don't! I'm so scared! Help me! Please help me! Please, please, please!'

As the desperate words poured from him, Usama had taken the old man's hand from his head and clasped it tight against his heaving chest.

For several minutes there was no sound but that of the boy's weeping and the night breeze sifting gently through the palm trees outside the open windows.

Eventually the old slave let out a long sigh of resignation. 'Yes, Usama, I believe it is the will of Allah that I try. My time has come and I will help you.'

So it was that as dawn was breaking, Old Mahmood was seen leaving his master's house and making his way swiftly down to the harbour. Here he talked earnestly with a Hindu sea captain, who was preparing to set out that morning on a voyage to Calicut in distant India. After a while the slave took out a small leather bag, handed some of its glittering contents to the captain, then retraced his steps to the house.

A few minutes later, the slave re-emerged escorting a woman, completely covered in black robes, as custom demanded of the wives of the rich, and went with her to the harbour. From the stonequay she stepped lightly onto the dhow of the Hindu captain, to whom Mahmood gave the remaining contents of his purse. After half an hour the ship edged away from the quay. With her broad lateen sail billowing in the breeze, she slid swiftly between the towers and was soon no more than a speck on the vast expanse of the Indian Ocean.

'Captain! Captain!' the urgent call cut through Abu Sebba's daydreaming, jolting him back to the present. He shook his head and glanced quickly about him.

'Yes, Abdullah?'

'Shall I lower the sail, Captain? I asked you about a dozen times afore but you seemed somewhere else and didn't hear me.'

'Yes, lower away, Mr Mate. My apologies. I

was somewhere else – in another time, rather.'

When the sail had been furled and neatly rolled away and the stately dhow was drifting slowly towards a berth at the quayside, Abu Sebba turned to the mate and asked thoughtfully, 'That skeleton, Abdullah . . . ?'

'Aye, Captain? What about it?'

'Tortured to death, I suppose?'

'So they say, Captain. The most painful execution they could dream up. It was to be a warning, they said, against others trying to help slaves escape.'

Abu Sebba wiped his sleeve hurriedly across his face. 'The usual practice. I don't suppose you know who the victim was, do you?'

'Of course I do, Captain. Everyone does. It's a famous story. The man was Old Mahmood, slave of one Ibn Massoud, and the person he helped to freedom was a young African boy named Usama. He went off to India in a ship and vanished without trace, they say.'

'Really!' mused Abu Sebba. 'Without trace, eh? Well, he was lucky!'

That night a great storm raged over the port.

The rain was so heavy and the wind so strong that all right-thinking folk, even the beggars and the guards who normally kept watch on the harbour towers in all weathers, stayed indoors. Yet one man did venture out, a tall fellow with curly hair. He was closely wrapped in a cloak against the storm and carried a canvas bag in his right hand.

The wind had all but blown itself out by morning. Emerging to see what damage had been done, the people of the town found uprooted trees, houses without roofs and stranded fish lying like ornaments in streets many paces from the sea. It was also discovered that the storm had even carried off the bones of Old Mahmood, which had grimly adorned the harbour towers for so many years.

Three days later, after his dhow had been unloaded and a fresh cargo stowed safely aboard, Abu Sebba guided his vessel out of the harbour and set a course for the south. When the craft was slipping along nicely before a following breeze, he went to the small hut in the stern that served as his cabin and emerged with a large canvas bag.

Very carefully, almost as if he were conducting

a religious ceremony, the captain lifted the bag and held it over the side of the ship. After muttering a few words, he dropped it into the sea and watched as it sank rapidly out of sight.

Abdullah the mate, who had been watching with rising curiosity, asked, 'Begging your pardon, Captain, but what was that?'

Abu Sebba turned and gave him a curious, contented smile. 'That? That, Mr Mate, was an old friend. The best I ever had. I was saying goodbye – and, yes, thanking him for saving my life.'

THE ARAB SLAVE TRADE

Arab merchants began to trade in slaves from East Africa in the seventh century and continued to do so for another 1300 years. Over that period, at least as many Africans were enslaved as in the better-known Atlantic slave trade. Captives were shipped back to the Middle East, where they were sold and given all kinds of menial work. The least fortunate were required as eunuchs. This involved a crude and cruel operation (the 'process' in this story) that had a survival rate of about 1 in 25.

THE VISION

Olaudah Equiano

T he night began so happily.

Seated around the blazing fire, we had feasted since the almighty sun slipped to rest beneath the dreaming forest. Pineapples as large as a man's head, spiced chicken steaming from the pot, yams, corn – my father honoured his son with the finest food we had. Then, after the feast, the palm wine flowed and we began to dance.

To the slow strum and throb of drums, armed men stamped and leaped in mock war while

Damla, the mightiest warrior of the tribe, recited a long poem about the hunt of the lion. Next came the ladies. Clad in azure robes and decked with clinking gold, they sang and swayed to rhythmic music that rose on the flames to mingle with the stars in the ebony canopy of the African night.

All this was for me. I looked across at my father and, sensing my gaze, he turned his head towards me. Giving me a smile of deep contentment, he raised his hand in salutation. He was so proud of me. His boy, Olaudah, the first born of the great chief, had spied the kidnappers as they climbed into our compound. He had raised the alarm. With great bravery, he had led the attack on the intruders, trapping them with ropes and holding them fast until the adults arrived.

It was for this deed, my first act as a warrior and leader, that my father had ordered the celebration. I returned his greeting by clasping my hands together and bowing my head. There is no finer feeling for a boy than to know that his father is proud of him. And I would make him prouder still, I resolved. I would learn to be fair and wise, like him, and I would lead the men in battle and I would—

A shriek slashed the air like a blade. The music stopped. All heads turned towards the bent and wizened figure trembling out of the shadows into the firelight. It was Namdami.

'Woe!' she cried, waving her scrawny arms about like a great bird trying to leave the ground. 'There are pictures before my eyes. Bright pictures! Terrible pictures!'

By now the whole tribe was sitting transfixed by the crone's eerie performance. Namdami had never been like this before. In fact, she had ventured out of her hut only rarely since the evening, several years before, when she had staggered in from the forest and begged for shelter. She had been travelling, she said, and was very weary. My father took pity on her and let her stay. Since then she had sometimes given advice on which herbs cured certain ailments, but otherwise she had kept herself to herself. She had never said where she had come from nor what she had done before she arrived. Being a well-mannered people, we had assumed it was a secret and had not asked her. If the truth be told, until this moment many of us had almost forgotten her existence.

Namdami took a few more hesitant steps, then suddenly knelt down on the ground and covered her face with her hands. For the first time I noticed she wore an enormous gold ring fashioned in the form of twisted snakes.

Speaking through her bony fingers, she began again in a piercing, high-pitched voice that was almost a scream. 'Red devils! Beware! Oh, beware, my children! They have seized you with hands – no, claws as those of the vulture. Carried, carried, carried through the forest like yams in a sack. Who is that man? He has gold in his hand, round gold. There is no escape! Poor children! Oh, the poor, poor children!'

By now it was clear to everyone what was going on. Namdami the Stranger was seeing a vision. We knew all about visions and we respected and feared them. Once, my mother said, one of our warriors had seen a vision of his own dead body and refused to go into battle. But while the fighting was taking place, he had trodden on a snake and died of its bite – showing that his vision had been real after all.

Never having met anyone who had actually seen a vision, I watched, fascinated, as Namdami continued with her chilling message. 'Chains there are,' she shrieked. 'Iron chains coming from their necks. Ohhh! What is that? What can I see?'

The prophetess slowly rose to her feet, taking her hands from her face as she did so. She was weeping and her tears made her wrinkled face shine in the firelight. 'Water! Water to the end of the world!' she said, speaking more quietly now and staring over our heads into the darkness. 'So much water! A house on the water, a house with wings! The children are going in, into the darkness. There is weeping . . . such pain! More red men – no! Strangers. Not red. White like clouds with black teeth. And the children . . . !'

At this point Namdami swung round and pointed a long, stick-like finger towards Armala, my younger sister. Trembling, the prophetess cried out in a terrible voice, 'You! It is you I have seen!'

Armala screamed and grabbed hold of our mother. I wanted to go and comfort her, but before I could do so Namdami had moved again. This time she was facing me. Horrified, I stared at the dark shape before me, at the thin bones, the wild hair, the eyes dull red like dying embers.

Once again the hand rose and the finger pointed.

'She is not alone. Her brother is with her, the noble Olaudah, the one who will be chief of his people. Not now! Oh no, not now! He will go to great water with the weeping Armala. The pain! The misery! It is too much . . . too much! Ayee!'

With a hideous wail, the ancient prophetess fell to the ground, clutching at her eyes. Her body twitched wildly, then she lay still. Namdami the Stranger was dead.

Namdami's prophecy was the talk of the village for weeks afterwards. For many nights my sister Armala and I could not sleep, and several times I was woken in the night by horrible nightmares. My mother was clearly shaken but my father dismissed the prophecy as the ranting of a mad old woman. 'She did not know our people,' he explained, 'so how could she see visions about them? Have no fear, children, and all will be well.'

Gradually, even our mother began to grow less anxious. The memories of that dreadful night slowly faded and life returned to normal. So why, you wonder, did I tell you about the prophecy in the first place?

I told you because it came true. About a year after Namdami's death, it happened, just as she had foretold. One afternoon three people from a tribe we knew as the 'Red People', a woman and two men, climbed over the walls of our compound and grabbed Armala and me before we could cry out. They gagged us and ran off into the woods, carrying us under their arms like pigs for the slaughter.

We were not slaughtered, although I wish we had been. We were tied in sacks and carried for many days before being sold to a tall, brown-faced gentleman with a bright blue cloth wrapped round his head and a pair of pistols in his belt. He locked us in chains and led us, together with twenty others he had bought, down a long muddy path to a great water, just as Namdami had described. It was the sea, although before then I had never even heard of such a thing.

On the sea floated Namdami's 'houses' – the great ships of the Europeans who had bought us from the trader with pistols in his belt. Crying and clinging to each other until we were torn apart, Armala and I were taken in irons to separate vessels. You cannot imagine my heart-breaking

misery or that of the others with whom I was locked in a dark, evil-smelling hold and shipped across the sea to the island where I am now.

I labour on a sugar plantation from sunrise to sunset. My owner's initials have been burned into my right arm with a red-hot branding iron. I am whipped if I disobey or misunderstand an order. My food is meagre, my family lost, my hopes crushed.

I am a slave.

OLAUDAH EQUIANO

Olaudah Equiano was born in Benin, West Africa, in about 1750. While still young, he and his sister were captured by African slavers. Olaudah was eventually sold to a British captain and transported to the West Indies to work as a plantation slave. Luck, hard work and great skill enabled him to buy his freedom. The account he later wrote of his life is one of the most famous 'slave narratives'.

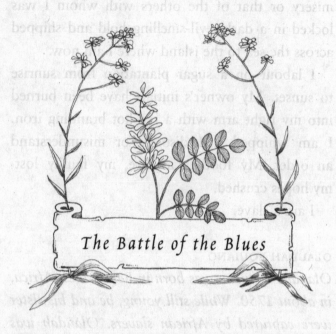

The Battle of the Blues

Back in the seventeenth century, the good citizens of St Lucie-sur-Oise knew their place. The boy who tended the abbey pigs on the edge of the forest knew that he must raise his coarse woollen cap to the pork butcher, and the pork butcher never failed to raise his smart three-cornered felt hat to the schoolmaster. And everyone, even elderly Father Gregory, raised their hats to Monsieur Grollier, manufacturer, merchant and patron of all worthy causes.

Claude Grollier's fortune – and a considerable one it was, too – came from woad. His fields grew the plants, his mills ground the leaves and his foul-smelling fermentation houses (situated several miles from his own dwelling) produced the precious blue dye which his pack horses then carried to markets. Here his employees sold it from his stalls to clothmakers large and small throughout France. It was rumoured locally that even royalty wore clothing coloured with the magnificent 'Grollier Blue'.

One might be forgiven for imagining that wealth and a little fame had made the hard-working merchant a contented man. It was not so. Fate had dealt him two cruel blows. Eighteen years previously, his dearest, most beloved Aurélie, the wife to whom he had been married for five delight-ful years, had died while giving birth to their third child, a daughter. No sooner had little Marjorianne been baptized than she, too, was carried off to another world. So the young businessman, almost beside himself with grief, was left with his money, ambition, two healthy sons – but no love.

As one might expect of a comparatively young man, from time to time Claude Grollier considered remarriage. Alas! He never got further than thinking about it. The idea of a wedding reminded him of Aurélie, which made him weep, and so that was the end of it. He therefore arranged for his two boys, Paul and Louis, to be raised by a succession of nurses, governesses and tutors until the age of sixteen, at which point they were destined to enter the family business.

It was clear from a very early age, when Paul was six and Louis scarcely more than four, that the younger boy was the brighter of the pair. By seven he could add up several columns of figures while his brother was still struggling with one, and his letters were so elegantly written that his proud father carried one around in his pocket to show his business friends.

'Now here's something special!' he would say, drawing the paper from his coat and spreading it out before him on the table. 'How old would you say the hand was that penned this?'

When the answers were all in, Claude Grollier would stick out his chest, beam around at the company like the great light at the entrance to Royan harbour, and declare that the hand was that of his younger son – his little Louis, only six years old! Rarely can there have been a prouder father.

Pride, as they say, comes before a fall, and so it was with Monsieur Claude Grollier, merchant in woad and associated dyes. Until he reached the age of thirteen, little Louis continued to soak up learning as a dog soaks up the spring sunshine. After that he seemed to slip into some sort of decline, becoming listless, failing to complete his compositions, half learning the languages his father and tutors pressed him with, and growing rude and surly in his manner. When his confused father tried beating the awkwardness out of his prodigy, he found that the punishment merely knocked it further in. In the end he gave up on the boy and left him to mope about the house while he went to work with his elder brother.

Whatever Paul Grollier lacked in wit, he made up for in other ways. He learned slowly but thoroughly. He worked like a plough horse all day and, if necessary, all night. He was polite, willing and extremely capable in practical matters like repairing a broken sail on a windmill or replacing the wooden rollers in a woad-crushing machine. By the time of his twenty-first birthday, Paul had almost as much knowledge of the family woad business as his father. He knew the markets and the men who worked there. To be doubly sure that he always had the facts at his fingertips, he kept a small pocketbook about him in which he wrote down the names of all the Grolliers' employees, their jobs, family, ages and wages.

It was this handy little book that led to the fight.

Returning home one rainy evening in November, Paul took the day's papers from his pockets and laid them on the writing table in the drawing room, ready to be worked on after supper. He then went upstairs to wash his hands and put on a clean shirt. While he was gone, Louis, now aged almost nineteen, rose from the chair where he had been reading a book and sauntered over to the table to inspect what his brother had dumped there.

After leafing through a few unimportant receipts, Louis's eyes fell on his brother's precious pocketbook. He picked it up and started to read. As he did so, his mouth spread into a broad grin and he emitted a snort of disbelieving laughter.

'What on earth do you need this for?' Louis asked when Paul re-entered the room.

Paul blushed. 'Leave it alone, Louis! It's none of your business!'

'Not true. It looks like the family business, and that includes me.'

'Ha!' scoffed Paul, tossing his head like a horse. 'Why should it include you when you show no interest in it at all? Lazing about all hours, never doing a day's decent work, while Father and I slave like Trojans.'

'I work, in my own way.'

'Oh yes? Go on then – what did you do today?'

'Met a sailor and had a chat. Read a book.'

'Met a sailor?! God's holy bones! Louis, I'm ashamed of you sometimes, I really am! How does talking to some drunken tar help the business?'

Louis's eyes narrowed slightly. 'He was not drunken, Paul. He was a captain and actually quite interesting. He told me important things none of us know. You don't have to work with your hands, like a peasant. Learning new things and thinking about them can be work, too – but you're too stupid to understand that!'

If there was one thing that made Paul angry, it was being reminded of those days in the schoolroom when his irritating younger brother had overtaken him in all subjects. He had laboured ever since to prove himself every bit as capable as Louis, and now that he had done so in his father's eyes, he was determined not to let the position slip.

'At least I'm not so stupid as to believe what sailors say!' Paul retorted sarcastically. 'What was it? Some mermaid story?'

Louis ignored the remark. Picking up his brother's pocketbook, he read in a deliberately slow voice, '*Mon-siuer de la Rue* – spelled wrong!'

Before he could continue, Paul sprang forward and snatched the book from Louis's hands. 'You're pathetic, you are!' he snarled. 'That's about all you can do, make clever-clever comments about people who actually get things done!'

Louis, usually so unemotional, was by now quite angry. 'Get things done? Well, a cow actually gets things done! That's about your level, isn't it? A cowpat maker!'

Paul, his lips pursed, was breathing heavily

through his nose. 'Say that again, scrounger!'

'Deaf as well, are you? I said you're as thick as a bone-headed cow!'

'Right!' Paul growled, advancing towards his brother. 'I've been wanting to do this for a very long time, Louis! You make me . . . sick!'

On the word 'sick', Paul swung a large right fist and smashed his brother to the floor. As he fell, Louis's head collided heavily with the table, bruising his cheek and knocking out one of his front teeth.

For a few seconds he lay in a daze as the blood oozed from his mouth and fell in large drops to the floor beside him. He eventually picked himself up and, with tears streaming from his eyes, wiped pathetically at the red mess staining the front of his white shirt.

'All right, Paul,' he spluttered, slowly shaking his head, 'I won't fight back with fists – it's not my way. I've thought for a long time that you and Father hate me, and now I know it. I'm leaving.'

Feeling horribly guilty at what he had done, Paul said quickly, 'No, I don't hate you, Louis. Nor does Father. It's just that—'

'Too late, Paul. I'm off. But I'll be back one day, I promise, and then you'll regret what you've done. I promise you will!'

Before his brother could say another word, Louis had left the room. Five minutes later, carrying a small leather bag, he left the house in which he had been born and in which he had spent the first eighteen years of his life, and walked quickly out into the night.

Twenty-five years passed. Monsieur Claude Grollier, a widower to the last, had died and in his will left his entire fortune and business to his son Paul. Of Louis, the lad who had walked out into the rain without saying goodbye, there was no mention at all.

In Paul's steady, capable hands the woad business went along nicely for a few years, then slowly began to decline. It took the owner a year or two to work out what was happening. His fields were as productive as ever, his crops as heavy. He paid his labourers no more than anyone else. His mills ran efficiently, and at the fairs and markets his dyes were displayed with skill. Yet still his sales went on falling.

His blue dye, it seemed, was just too expensive.

For five years Paul sold his dye for less than the cost of making it. He made up the loss from his personal fortune. When this ran out, he had to put his prices up again. As before, sales tumbled. He tried selling some of his mills but, having heard what was happening, no one wanted to buy them. Eventually, to save money, Paul took to working in the markets himself, standing behind a stall in all weathers like an ordinary shopkeeper.

It was while he was working at the Cahors fair that Paul Grollier finally discovered the reason for his difficulties. A Spanish cloth merchant, previously an important customer, inspected the Grollier dye and congratulated Paul on its quality. Yet he would not be buying any, he confessed. He could get good blue dye at about half the price elsewhere. Swallowing his pride, the despairing manufacturer asked where this 'elsewhere' might be.

'Bordeaux,' replied the Spaniard. Everyone went there to buy their blue dye nowadays. But Bordeaux was a wine town, Paul observed, miles from the woad fields and mills. The Spaniard shrugged. All he knew was that if you wanted blue dye, the place to buy it was not a traditional market like Cahors or Toulouse but in Bordeaux.

So the next day Paul packed up his stall, sent the unsold produce back home and set off for the great Atlantic port. On his arrival, he enquired where he could purchase blue dye. The docks, he was told, and when he got there he should ask for Monsieur L'Indien.

Paul followed these directions and soon found himself knocking at the door of a large, modern mansion close to the waterfront. A brown-faced servant in Indian clothes greeted him politely and asked him in perfect French to wait in an elegant reception room, where Monsieur L'Indien would soon attend him.

A minute or so later, a door clicked open behind Paul and, as he turned to see who it was, a familiar voice said, 'Brother, at last! I have been waiting so long for you to come and see me!'

If Paul could not believe his ears, his eyes scarcely made sense either. Gone was the Louis he last remembered, the scrawny, lisping youth with streaming eyes and a bloody mouth. In his place stood an elegant gentleman dressed entirely as an Indian, with a turquoise silk turban on his head and fingers aflame with emeralds and rubies.

'Louis!' cried Paul, suddenly feeling shabby and low and guilty all at the same time. 'I didn't know . . . I mean, how do you . . . ? What has happened?'

Over the next few days Louis Grollier, who ran his business as Monsieur L'Indien, gradually told his story. It began, he explained, with the conversation he'd had with the sea captain the day he left home. The man had recently returned from India. Here he had learned of a plant named indigo that produced a blue dye just as good as that from woad, but with half the effort. Louis had been going to discuss this news with his father and brother but had changed his mind after the row with Paul. Instead, he had sailed to India and learned for himself all about the manufacture of indigo dye. Using the skills picked up from his father, he had then set up his own indigo business and sold the dye in

France for half the price of that made from woad.

'And so I suppose I have kept my departing promise to you,' said Louis with a smile that revealed a complete set of white teeth. 'Although I am sorry for the hardship you have suffered.'

'It's amazing!' gasped Paul. 'You are now richer than Father ever was!'

'And there's enough to keep you and your family in comfort, too, Paul. Don't worry, I have forgotten our little argument – and forgiven you for the tooth.'

Embarrassed, Paul apologized for perhaps the fiftieth time for losing his temper and striking out at his brother on that dark November evening all those years ago. 'Yet perhaps it helped you in the long run,' he smiled, putting his hand on Louis's shoulder. 'If I hadn't hit you, you wouldn't have left home and made your fortune. Why, you've even managed to grow a new tooth!'

'Not new – ivory!' laughed Louis, tapping the gleaming white peg with his fingernail. 'Fitted by an Indian craftsman of remarkable skill. I tell you, brother, there is no limit to the wonders of the Orient!'

WOAD AND INDIGO

The blue dye used to colour European cloth traditionally came from the woad plant. The process was slow, smelly and difficult. From the sixteenth century onwards, dye from Indian indigo plants became widely available. Because this was easier and cheaper to produce, Europe's woad industry fell into decline. Despite the efforts of 'Woadite' merchants to protect their business, it eventually disappeared altogether. In the nineteenth century, chemical dyes killed off indigo production. Recently, manufacturers have begun to look again at natural dyes from woad and indigo because they do not harm the environment.

eden project

Deep in a giant crater in Cornwall are the two biggest greenhouses in the world – the famous Biomes of the Eden Project, where you can enter a lush tropical rainforest or the dry, scented lands of the Mediterranean.

They were created to show people just how much we depend on plants to feed and clothe us. You can see for yourself the trees and fruits and flowers that become chocolate, baked beans, rubber tyres, cotton T-shirts, paper for books and much more.

You can discover plants at Eden through music, art and storytelling – and through Eden Project books too!

www.edenproject.com

FANTASTIC TALES OF TRUE-LIFE ADVENTURERS!

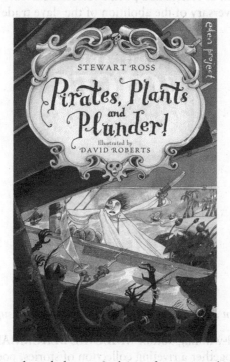

Travelling the globe searching for new plants is no easy task. Fighting off pirate attacks and outwitting bears, surviving kidnap, starvation and disgusting diets – such perils are all in a day's work for the true-life adventurers in this sparkling collection of stories. Meet famous voyagers like Magellan, Cortes and Columbus, and discover the extraordinary stories behind the plants we use every day!

Available now as an Eden Project paperback

ISBN: 978 1 903 91935 4

FOR OLDER READERS:

A collection of stories and poems to commemorate the 200th anniversary of the abolition of the slave trade act.

Slavery – an inhuman trade in human misery and suffering . . .

Award-winning author **MALORIE BLACKMAN** has drawn together a riveting collection of stories, poems and first-hand recollections on the theme of slavery.

JOHN AGARD
OLAUDAH EQUIANO
ALEX HALEY
and
BENJAMIN ZEPHANIAH

are among those whose work appears alongside an original story and foreword from Malorie herself.

Honour the past – and look forward towards a future in which all peoples of the world may live together in freedom.

Available now as a CORGI paperback
ISBN: 978 0 552 55600 2